HOLINESS, SPEECH AND SILENCE

*A richly pondered work of mature insight, brilliantly
written and easily accessible.*
David Martin, Emeritus Professor, LSE.

*This book beautifully distils central themes in
reflections on what Christian faith is about, whether
you are a Christian or an interested bystander. There
is a simplicity and directness which readers cannot but
find attractive. This is wonderful theology for people
who think theology is not for them; either because it
is too technical or because it is barely Christian.
Nicholas Lash is always a joy to read.*
Fergus Kerr OP, Blackfriars, Oxford

The late Cornelius Ernst once said that Aquinas' 'Five
Ways' were 'an attempt to show how we may go on
speaking of God in the ordinary world'.

Nicholas Lash shows how the main contours of the
Christian doctrine of God may be mapped onto
principal features of our culture and its predicaments.
After an introductory chapter on 'The Question of God
Today', Nicholas Lash considers – in chapters entitled
'Globalization and Holiness', 'Cacophony and
Conversation' and 'Attending to Silence' – three
dimensions of our contemporary predicament:
globalization, a crisis of language, and the pain and
darkness of the world, in relation to the doctrine of
God as Spirit, Word and Father.

HOLINESS, SPEECH AND SILENCE

Reflections on the Question of God

NICHOLAS LASH
University of Cambridge

ASHGATE

Published by
Ashgate Publishing Limited   Ashgate Publishing Company
Gower House   Suite 420
Croft Road   101 Cherry Street
Aldershot   Burlington, VT 05401-4405
Hampshire GU11 3HR   USA
England

Ashgate website: http://www.ashgate.com

British Library Cataloguing in Publication Data
Lash, Nicholas
 Holiness, speech and silence : reflections on the question of God
 1. God – Attributes
 I. Title
 231'.044

Library of Congress Cataloging-in-Publication Data
Lash, Nicholas.
 Holiness, speech and silence : reflections on the question of God / Nicholas Lash.
  p. cm.
 Includes index.
 ISBN 0-7546-5180-0 (hardcover : alk. paper)
 – ISBN 0-7546-5039-1 (pbk : alk. paper)
  1. God. 2. Trinity. 3. Catholic Church–Doctrines. 4. Christian sociology–Catholic Church. I. Title.

 BT103.L37 2004
 231–dc22

                                                  2004006131

ISBN 0 7546 5180 0 (HBK)
ISBN 0 7546 5039 1 (PBK)

Typeset in Sabon by Owain Hammonds, Ceredigion.
Printed by MPG Books Ltd, Bodmin, Cornwall.

Contents

Foreword

The lectures of which this little book is an expanded version first saw the light of day as the Prideaux Lectures, which I had the honour to deliver in the University of Exeter in the spring of 2002. I gave them again, in a slightly revised version, in Westminster Cathedral Hall during Lent 2004, as my contribution to the tenth-anniversary celebrations of the establishment of the Margaret Beaufort Institute in Cambridge. I am extremely grateful to Professor Gorringe and his colleagues at Exeter; to Sister Bridget Tighe and her colleagues at the Margaret Beaufort Institute, and to the authorities at Westminster Cathedral, for their invitations and encouragement; and to the staff at Ashgate Publishing for the skill and conscientiousness with which they brought the text to publication.

One kind person, on reading the manuscript, expressed regret that I 'never actually discuss trinitarian doctrine'. The Canadian theologian Bernard Lonergan is said to have begun a course of lectures on the doctrine of the Trinity as follows: 'In the most blessed Trinity, there are five notions, four relations, three persons, two processions, one nature and, some would say, no problem.' This book takes the shape that it does, not because I wish to evade those technicalities which have, undoubtedly, their proper time and place, but because it is not, in my experience, by way of the technical 'grammar' of the matter that most people are brought to some understanding of what the doctrine means.

Nicholas Lash

Silence and music

Silence, come first. I see a sleeping swan,
Wings closed and drifting where the water leads.
A winter moon, a grove where shadows dream,
A hand outstretched to gather hollow reeds.
The four winds in their litanies can tell
All of earth's stories as they weep and cry,
The sea names all the treasure of her tides,
The birds rejoice between the earth and sky.
Voices of grief and from the heart of joy;
So near to comprehension do we stand
That wind and sea and all of winged delight
Lie in the octaves of man's voice and hand
And music wakes from silence, where it slept.
Ursula Wood

(Set to music by her husband Ralph Vaughan Williams.)

With kind permission of Albion Music Ltd.

Chapter 1

The Question of God Today

What Does God Look Like?

I remember a conversation, over forty years ago, with a friend of mine, a retired primary school teacher. She was extremely angry. Her small grand-daughter, aged six or seven, had just come back from school, in some distress. An idiotic teacher had told the class to draw a picture of God. The school was in Marlow, an attractive small town on the Thames, about thirty miles upstream from London. The little girl had drawn a picture of a swan, sailing serenely along among the rushes. The teacher, on seeing it, berated her, complaining: 'That's not what God looks like!'

All one's sympathies, of course, are with the child – who had, presumably, provided what, in today's jargon, we might call an 'icon' of majesty and beauty. But what, one wonders, was the teacher looking for? What did she think God looks like?

This might, at first sight, seem to be a foolish question because, since God is generally agreed to be invisible, there is presumably nothing whatsoever that God could 'look' like. And yet, however much we emphasize that everything we say of God is metaphorically said; however much we insist that the holy mystery which we call 'God' absolutely outstrips, not merely our imagination but our understanding; when people talk of God – whether they do so as atheists, agnostics or devout believers; whether as

Christians, Jews, Muslims or Hindus; whether or not, in speaking about God, they mentally capitalize the letter 'G' – they usually suppose themselves to have *some* idea of what they are talking about. And, whatever one is talking about, if one has got some idea of what one is talking about, then – however general, vague, confused, that idea may be – there is *some* sort of story one could tell about it; some picture one could paint, however broad the brushstrokes that one used.

What, then, might God look like? Here's another little parable, from Salley Vickers' splendid novel about Venice and the Book of Tobit, *Miss Garnet's Angel*. Tobias is talking to his guide Azarias (better known to us, although not yet, at this point in the story, to Tobias, as the archangel Raphael):

> 'Azarias', I said: 'You told me once I may find out who or what you worshipped when we got to Ecbatana. Might you tell me now?'. 'How would courage and truth and mercy and right action strike you?' 'But those are not gods!' I protested. 'Tobias, for heaven's sake, what do you think a god looks like when he works in men?'[1]

That exchange suggests, first, that, when thinking about God or (shall we say) considering what God looks like, we should be thinking about what people worship and, second, that, when thinking about what people worship, we should perhaps be thinking, not so much about 'things' – objects, entities, individuals – but rather about occurrences, activities, patterns of behaviour. Courage and truth and mercy are displayed (or not displayed) in the ways that we behave, in what we do. More generally, it is only through what we do and undergo that what we *are* is shown and known. We should not, perhaps, rule out the possibility that something similar may be true of God.

A few years ago, a survey was conducted amongst seventeen-year-olds in the Czech Republic. Only one per cent of those interviewed were skinheads, but eight per cent knew what skinheads were *about*. Only fifteen per cent said that they were Christians. Readers presuming that to be bad news should brace themselves for worse: the percentage of those interviewed who knew what Christianity was about was – fifteen!

We underestimate at our peril the comprehensiveness of the ignorance of Christianity in contemporary Western cultures. At least the teenagers of Prague seemed to know that they did *not* know what Christianity is about. My guess is that, for most people in Britain, ignorance takes the more intractable form of supposing that 'everybody knows' what Christianity is, and that 'everybody knows' that it is false: at best, a fairytale less engaging than *The Lord of the Rings*; at worst, a child's comforter clung to by those lacking the courage to face the bleakness of existence.

This state of affairs has not, of course, come about overnight. Here is Cardinal Newman writing, as an old man, in 1882, to a friend of his – a barrister who had previously spent some years in the Madras Civil Service: the

> primary and special office of religion men of the world do not see, and they see only its poverty as a principle of secular progress, and, as disciples and upholders and servants of that great scientific progress, they look on religion and despise it ... I consider then that it is not reason that is against us, but imagination. The mind, after having, to the utter neglect of the Gospels, lived in science, experiences, on coming back to Scripture, an utter strangeness in what it reads, which seems to it a better argument against Revelation than any formal proof. 'Christianity' [it says] 'is behind the age'.[2]

Reason, Imagination and the Importance of Theology

'It is not reason that is against us, but imagination.' That is the point. The ways in which we 'see' the world, its story and its destiny; the ways in which we 'see' what human beings are, and what they're for, and how they are related to each other and the world around them; these things are shaped and structured by the stories that we tell, the cities we inhabit, the buildings in which we live, and work, and play; by how we handle – through drama, art and song – the things that give us pain and bring us joy. What does the world look like? What do we look like? What does God look like? It is not easy to think Christian thoughts in a culture whose imagination, whose ways of 'seeing' the world and everything there is to see, are increasingly unschooled by Christianity and, to a considerable and deepening extent, quite hostile to it.

In such a situation, continuing to hold the Gospel's truth makes much more serious and dangerous demands than mere lip-service paid to undigested information. Unless we make that truth our own through thought, and pain, and argument – through prayer and study and an unflinching quest for understanding – it will be chipped away, reshaped, eroded, by the power of an imagining fed by other springs, tuned to quite different stories. And this unceasing, strenuous, vulnerable attempt to make some Christian sense of things, not just in what we say, but through the ways in which we 'see' the world, is what is known as doing theology.[3]

And yet, in my experience, most Christians in Britain take a different view. I never cease to be astonished by the number of devout and highly educated Christians, experts on their own 'turf' as teachers, doctors, engineers, accountants, or whatever; regular readers of the broadsheet press and at least occasional browsers through the *Economist* or the *New Statesman*, the *New Scientist* or the *Times Literary Supplement*; occasional visitors to the theatre who usually read at least one of the novels on the Booker short-list; and who nevertheless, from one year to the next, never take up a serious work of Christian theology and probably suppose *The Tablet* to be something that you get from Boots the chemist.

It is, of course, perfectly true that erudition, or even literacy, are not necessary conditions of that aspect of holiness which is Christian wisdom. Nevertheless, ignorance is never virtuous, nor is the refusal to engage all the resources of the mind and heart at the service of faith's quest for understanding. It is difficult to avoid the conclusion that devout and educated Christians who refuse to acquire a theological competence cognate to the general level of their education simply do not care about the truth of Christianity or, at the very least, do not care sufficiently to seek some understanding of that Word through whom all things are made, into whose light we have been called, and which will set us free.[4]

I hope that these somewhat provocative remarks will not be dismissed as merely the disgruntled observations of an elderly academic who wishes that more people would buy his books! I have given quite a lot of thought as to why it is that the study of theology is as comprehensively marginalized from educated public discourse as it is in most Western countries and, while I am quite willing to concede that theologians must bear some share of the responsibility for this, I do think that some of the deeper reasons are to be sought in a systemic failure of the Christian churches to understand themselves as *schools* of Christian wisdom: as richly endowed projects of lifelong education.

What follows is a very broad-brush sketch of how, as I see it, this marginalization of theology has come about in Western culture during the past four centuries, and the impact that the process has had on Christian understanding. I shall do this under three headings: 'Changing the Subject', 'The Changing Nature of God' and 'The Changing Nature of Belief in God'. Then, in the following three chapters, I shall consider aspects of our contemporary predicament: globalization, a crisis of language, and the pain and darkness of the world, from the standpoint of the question of God understood as a question about holiness, and speech, and silence. (Those three motifs, it will be noticed, have something in common with Christian confession of faith in one known as Holy Spirit, and as Word, and as the originating stillness in which that Word is spoken.)

Changing the Subject

It sometimes happens, in the history of a word or phrase, that what was once what we might call the 'home territory' of its usage, its primary or central sense, atrophies or weakens until some quite other sense – which, in the beginning, either did not exist at all or was, at most, entirely marginal – moves centre stage, takes over and makes itself at home. And, when this happens, it will often be very difficult, perhaps impossible, straightforwardly or spontaneously to recapture, or even to imagine, the way in which the expression was originally used.

Consider, for example, the word 'invention'. When this word first appears in English, some time in the fourteenth century (the first occurrence listed in the *Oxford English Dictionary* dates from 1350), it carries the same sense as the Latin verb – *invenio, invenire* – which it translates. Invention is a matter of coming upon something, discovering or finding it. Within two hundred years, other senses have been derived from this: by the 1530s, for example, it is possible to invent something, find it, come upon it, without ever leaving your armchair, simply by working it out or making a plan. Occasionally, the usage is pejorative: to charge someone with 'inventing' something may, by the mid-sixteenth century, be to accuse them of making it up, of telling lies: in Coverdale's translation of 1535, Susanna defends herself against the elders: 'I never did any such things, as these men have maliciously invented against me.'[5]

And it is this originally marginal, derived sense, or something very like it, which moved to centre stage, to the extent that, if someone who knew nothing of the history of the expression came across a somewhat old-fashioned liturgical calendar, they would be quite baffled by the Church's celebration of 'The Invention of the Cross'. What on earth, they might well wonder, was Helena, mother of the Emperor Constantine, *up to*? How could a woman, even one of royal blood, who died some two hundred years after the Crucifixion, possibly have 'invented' the Cross of Christ (except in the sense that few historians, these days, would be quite sure that she found it)?

In this case, the usurpation of the home territory of the meaning of 'invention' by a later sense originally entirely derivative and marginal, has done no great harm: we have plenty of other ways of expressing the process of coming upon things, finding or discovering them (although there is perhaps a sense in which Christopher Columbus 'invented' America).

But, to move from an actual to a fictional example, imagine a state of affairs in which the word 'love', and all its cognates, had ceased to be used, by anyone, to say things like 'I love you' or 'We love each other' – expressions (originally the primary and central uses of the word 'love') which those using them had known how dangerous it was to use them carelessly; had known how vulnerable the users were to the risks of their misuse. Imagine, that is to say, a situation in which the word 'love' was now *only* used, as it were, at a distance, in the derived and secondary territory of reported speech. In stark contrast to the risks – to one's identity, responsibility and history – of serious, self-involving use of the simple confession: 'I love you', think how little is invested by the speaker in a statement such as: 'Queen Victoria deeply loved Prince Albert'.

If, *per impossibile*, it were ever thus to happen that the primary and central confessional, self-involving uses of the word 'love' and its cognates were to be rendered practically and imaginatively almost irrecoverable, human existence – we would, I think, agree – would have been thereby devastatingly, perhaps terminally, impoverished.

You may well think that this example is so far-fetched as not to have been worth concocting (or inventing!). And yet, I now want to argue that something not entirely dissimilar has happened, in Western cultures, during the past four hundred years, to the word 'God'.

Few changes in the character, or structure, of the ways in which we understand, imagine, think about ourselves, the world, its history and all that's in it, have been more comprehensive, or had more far-reaching consequences, than the change from late medieval to early modern Western culture. At one level, we can tell the story of the change as a shift in imaginative and intellectual ambition. Finding themselves in the dark, on a long and dangerous journey, medieval people tried to find out where to go and how to get there. Seeking their way home (for they knew themselves to be in exile) the intellectual dimension of their quest can be summed up as a search for *understanding*. And the search for understanding is, for all people and at all times, an *endless* search: whoever you are, and however wise and learned you may be, there is always infinitely more that you might try to understand.

Early modern man – and, in the context of this thumbnail sketch or caricature, I doubt if any feminist who knows the history of the Renaissance would object to the expression – was in search of certainty and power. He wanted firm ground beneath his feet (his *own* feet, because standing on one's own two feet, without assistance from unreliable so-called 'authorities', became, increasingly, part of his ambition) and, as it were, a mountain-peak on which to stand. He sought an *explanation* of the world, its intellectual *mastery*.

Explanation, unlike understanding, if successful comes to an end. Explanations are stories of causes and effects. Why is there a damp patch on the ceiling? Because water is dripping through from the floor above. Why is there water dripping through? Because that blasted child let the bath overflow. End of story. End of explanation. Problem solved. Even in these supposedly 'post-modern' times, the totalitarian ambition of 'complete' explanation, of a comprehensively explanatory 'theory of everything', of becoming, intellectually, 'masters of the universe', still lingers on in certain scientific circles.[6]

Where does God come into all this? During the seventeenth and eighteenth centuries, the word 'god' came to be used, for the first time, to name the ultimate explanation of the system of the world. And, when it was in due time realized that the system of the world was such as not to require any such single, overarching, independent, explanatory principle, the word 'god' was dispensed with, and modern 'atheism' was born. (There you have, in two sentences, the argument of Michael Buckley's learned and impressive study *At the Origins of Modern Atheism*.[7])

The Changing Nature of God

Against this general background of the comprehensive transformation from pre-modern into modern culture, I now turn in a little more detail to what I have called 'the changing nature of god'. In a nutshell, my argument will be that 'gods' which, before modernity, were understood to be whatever people worshipped, became, instead, beings of a particular kind – a 'divine' kind, we might say. And there are analogies between this usurpation of *worship* by *description* as the 'home territory' of uses of the word 'god' and my fictional parable of what might one day happen to uses of the word 'love'. (Incidentally, if 'gods' are now beings of a particular kind, then Christians, Jews, Muslims and atheists all have this, at least, in common: that *none* of them believe in gods.)

For most of our history, then, 'gods' were what people worshipped. I do not mean that people worshipped things called 'gods'; I mean that the word 'god' simply signified whatever it is that someone worships. In other words, the word 'god' worked rather like the way in which the word 'treasure' still does. A treasure is what someone treasures, what someone highly values. And I can only find out what you value by asking you and by observing your behaviour. Some people value reputation, some a quiet life. The point is that there is no class of objects known as 'treasures'. There is no use going into a supermarket and asking for six bananas, a loaf of bread, two packets of soap and three treasures. Valuing is a *relationship*: treasures are what we value.

Similarly, 'gods' are what people worship, have their hearts ultimately set on. I can only find out what you worship, what your gods are, by asking you and by observing your behaviour. And, these days, it is almost certain that the gods you worship will not be *named* by you as gods. Most of us are polytheists, inconsistently and confusingly worshipping ourselves, our country, 'freedom', sex or money. There is no class of objects known as 'gods'. Worshipping is a *relationship*: gods are what we worship.

Even at this stage in the story, two notes of caution need to be sounded. In the first place, there are, of course, degrees of valuing: you can value something very highly indeed, or you can value it a little. Are there, similarly, degrees of 'worshipping'? In point of terminology, clearly the answer is 'Yes', otherwise people in local government would spend a great deal of time confusing the Creator and Redeemer of the world with the local mayor (who is formally addressed as 'Your worship'). And so every tradition comes up with ways of distinguishing the worship due to the Creator and Redeemer of the world from the various forms of reverence, estimation, acknowledgement of worth ('worth-ship') differently due to creatures. The worship due to God, of course, goes far beyond mere reverence. It is, in its ambition, the total and absolute surrender of the self, acknowledgement of sheer contingency: ourselves and all things given back to the eternal giving which they express and celebrate. I would go so far as to say that the great religious traditions of the world are best understood as *schools*, contexts of education, the participants in which help each other thus to worship, while yet not worshipping any thing: not the world, nor any constituent fact or feature of the world; not any individual or ideal; not any nation, dream, event or memory.

My second cautionary note concerns a disturbing carelessness that is widespread in contemporary writing on the subject of religion. We live in a society the intellectual movers and shakers of which increasingly take it for granted that only children and the simple-minded still believe in God (Christianity is, as Newman said, deemed to be 'behind the age'). Nevertheless, when writing about cultures other than their own, these educated secularists will tell you a great deal about other peoples' 'gods'. Indians, especially, are said to worship many gods. Notice the racism implicit in this description: most Indians, it implies, are either infantile or simple-minded. According to my Cambridge colleague Julius Lipner, who has studied Hinduism more closely than most people in Britain, the Sanskritic tradition has never, in fact, advocated polytheism.[8] (Incidentally, the term 'polytheism' was first coined, in the seventeenth century, by an English Protestant, as a way of indicating that Indian ritual practices were really no better than the superstitions of Catholicism!)

In other words, if the first point to be made is that the fundamental and primary uses of the concept of God are *relational* – 'gods' are what we worship – the second point to be made is that elementary courtesy, to say nothing of concern for truth, requires us to pay continually discriminate attention as to which words well translate as 'god' and which do not, and as to which patterns of behaviour do and do not count, and in what sense, as instances of 'worship'. (A similar problem arises from the insouciance with which English-speaking people in the nineteenth century presumed that there must be some word in every other language that corresponded to the sense which the word 'religion' had newly come to acquire. Thus the Sanskrit word '*dharma*' was mistranslated as 'religion', and intractably deep misunderstanding between Indians and English-speaking Westerners was guaranteed.[9])

The confusion arises, of course, because those who write so carelessly about other peoples' gods simply take for granted that the word 'god' names a natural kind, a class of entity. There are bananas, traffic lights, human beings, and gods. Or perhaps not: on this account of how the word 'god' works, 'theists' are people who suppose the class of gods to have at least one member; 'monotheists' are those who maintain that the class has one, and only one, member; and 'atheists' are those who think that, in the real world, the class of 'gods' is, like the class of 'unicorns', empty. (It should not, by now, surprise the reader to learn that *all* these words – 'atheism', 'theism', 'monotheism', 'polytheism' – were first invented in the seventeenth century.)

One further complication: as the 'primary grammar' of the concept of God shifted from the relational language of praise and worship, of *address*, to the derived and secondary territory of description, the situation unfolded rather differently in English- and in German-speaking culture. I said earlier that, during the seventeenth and eighteenth centuries, the word 'god' came to name the ultimate explanatory principle of the system of the world. 'God', we might say, ceased to be the subject of what Thomas Aquinas had called 'holy teaching', and became, instead, in Britain, a topic in 'mechanics' or, as we would say these days, physics – the scientific study of the system of the world.

In German culture, things went rather differently, the Germans being less interested in machinery than in deep thought. German metaphysics, from Kant to Heidegger, became an immensely impressive exercise in substituting philosophy for theology, pure thought for prayerful reflection. Way back in the eleventh century, Saint Anselm had written two small books: one called *Monologion* or 'monologue', the other *Proslogion* or 'dialogue', 'response-speech'. Philosophy is of the first kind, theology of the second. Many of the great modern German thinkers supposed themselves to be *developing* the traditions of Christian thought into the circumstances of the modern world, whereas they were, in fact, subverting it, substituting for theology a quite different enterprise.

In 1807, Hegel published an immensely influential work entitled, in German, *Phänomenologie des Geistes*. A translation published in 1977 rendered this as *Phenomenology of Spirit* ('geist', 'ghost', 'spirit' – get it?), whereas, in 1931, an earlier translator had preferred *Phenomenology of Mind*. Was Hegel trying to give expression to the history of thought, or was he trying to realize the history of God? And how clear, to him, would this distinction have been? Did he, perhaps, presume these two histories, two processes, to be identical?

There are so many words around – big, abstract, misty words like 'absolute' and 'spirit'; 'the sublime', 'transcendence', 'power' and 'being' – the use of which disguises from our view the depth of the gulf which separates the monologues of modern metaphysics from those endlessly demanding, strenuously self-involving exercises in prayerful reflection which have characterized, in their different ways, the theologies of the great religious traditions of the world.

When talking about God, what difference does it make to spell it with a capital or a lower-case initial letter? Not a lot, one would have thought: bread and butter are still butter and bread, whichever word comes at the beginning of the sentence. What has happened, of course, is that we have got into the habit of imagining that 'God' (with a capital 'G') is the proper name of the object of our worship. Common names are names of members of a class: 'tree' names all the things that count as trees. Proper names are names proper to individual members of a class: all the readers of this text are human beings, but I am, I think, the only Nicholas Langrishe Alleyne Lash. But the incomprehensible and holy mystery we worship is not, I have been urging, a member of *any* class.

Each of the great religious traditions of the world has had its own procedures for protecting us from the illusion that the Holy One can be thus pinned down, classified, given a proper name. When Moses stands before the burning bush and asks: 'If I go to the Israelites and tell them that the God of their forefathers has sent me to them, and they ask me his name, what I shall say?', he receives an answer which more or less boils down to: 'Mind your own business!'[10] (It is, incidentally, this mysterious reply, sometimes translated as: 'I am who I am', which Aquinas quotes at the beginning of the discussion usually known as 'the Five Ways', in which his aim is not, as modern philosophy misleadingly puts it, to 'prove that God exists', to establish that there is a god, but rather to consider the sense in which 'existence-talk' is or is not appropriate here. When asking whether God 'exists', the question which concerns him is rather more like the question: 'do numbers "exist"?' than it is like the question: 'do unicorns exist?')[11]

But, if God has no proper name, how may we speak of Him? By discriminating amongst the innumerable names that we *might* use for Him. Much recent writing has given the impression that there are *two* kinds of theology: one kind, which says things about God, using what one writer has called 'concrete anthropomorphic imagery', and which is good enough, apparently, for the simple-minded people who still go to church; and another, more 'austere', sophisticated kind, known as 'negative' theology, which denies the appropriateness of the things that the simple-minded say. This latter way of doing things is sometimes attributed to an esoteric tribe known as 'mystics'.[12]

This, of course, is nonsense. Everything that human beings say of God, of the incomprehensible and holy mystery confessed by Christians to be Creator and Redeemer of the world, is said in words and images carved from the fabric of the world which the Creator makes. We have no other materials to use, no other way to think, or speak, or act. In this sense, everything that is said of God, whether by way of affirmation or denial, is anthropomorphically expressed.

The language that we use, the terminology that we employ, does not become *less* anthropomorphic, less sprung from earthly soil, by becoming more abstract, rarefied, or technical. If anything, something more like the opposite is the case: the entire Bible bears witness to the fact that the imagery of the poet and the storyteller is better fitted than the abstractions of the philosopher to express the relations that obtain between the Holy One and the creation which He convenes and calls into His presence.

In saying this, it is not in any way my intention to disparage the indispensable contribution of rigorous

philosophical reflection. The point is that *everything*
we say of God, whatever our style or register of
discourse, is anthropomorphically, metaphorically said,
and that, perhaps paradoxically, habits of speech
which, as it were, carry their metaphorical character on
their sleeve, may be *less* likely than more abstract
expressions to lead us into the trap of supposing that
now, at last, we are getting nearer to getting a 'fix' on
God, to grasping 'what God looks like'.[13]

'Oh, I *see*: God is "spirit", God is "transcendent",
God is "ineffable" – *now* I understand.' Oh no you
don't! Or, at least, you are probably better set upon the
road to understanding if you sing, with the psalmist,
that God covers himself with light as with a garment,
makes the clouds his chariot, and rides upon the wings
of the wind (see Ps. 104: 2–3) or, with Martin Luther,
that 'a mighty fortress is our God'. Images of
strengthening and power, of sovereignty and weakness,
of suffering and joy: these are good tools to take to
school in quest of ever less inappropriate speech
because, amongst other things, they remind us that to
speak appropriately of God is always, at the same
time, to speak appropriately of the world which God
creates, and of our place and duties in that process of
creation.

Where creatures are concerned, it is possible to
distinguish between, on the one hand, the kinds of
things best thought of as what were once called
'substances': 'chunky' things, we might say, enduring
over time – such as cities, trees and rock formations,
porpoises and people – and, on the other, things such as
movements and events, actions and occurrences, the
things we do and undergo, aspects of the ceaseless
movement which constitutes our ever-changing world.
Which kind of thing does the word 'God', as used by
Christians (who know that God is not a 'thing' of *any*
kind), attempt to mention? Which is the more
misleading: to speak of God as we might speak of

substances and people, or as we might speak of events and movements and occurrences (such as 'speaking', for example)?

I raise this question as a reminder that it may be well worth noticing that Thomas Aquinas (amongst many other theologians in the past) took very seriously the suggestion that 'the word "God" might actually be better regarded grammatically as a verb'[14] rather than a noun. I shall return to this suggestion in the next chapter.

It is, and always has been, exceedingly difficult to speak sensibly of God. The attempt is, nevertheless, required of every Christian – in response to the one Word which God is, and which has been spoken to us. There are not now, nor have there ever been, two theologies: one 'positive', the other 'negative'. The negative way, the '*via negativa*', is simply the endless and endlessly demanding *disciplining* of language and imagination which we need. Newman put it rather well in a paper on 'Certainty, Intuition and the Conceivable' which he wrote in 1863, and which remained unpublished in his lifetime:

> We can only speak of Him, whom we reason about but have not seen, in the terms of our experience. When we reflect on Him and put into words our thoughts about Him, we are forced to transfer to a new meaning ready made words, which primarily belong to objects of time and place. We are aware, while we do so, that they are inadequate, but we have the alternative of doing so, or doing nothing at all. We can only remedy their insufficiency by confessing it. We can do no more than put ourselves on the guard as to our own proceeding, and protest against it, while we do adhere to it. We can only set right one error of expression by another. By this method of antagonism we steady our minds, not so as to reach their object, but to point them in the right direction ... by saying and unsaying, to a positive result.[15]

The Changing Nature of Belief in God

If what I have called the 'primary grammar' of the concept of God, that sense of the way the word works which most people in our culture simply take for granted, has, as I have suggested, undergone a fundamental shift or sea-change – from 'god' as 'whatever it is that you worship', whatever it is on which your heart is ultimately set, to 'god' as the name of a kind or class of entities of which there may or may not, in the real world, be any members – then we might expect that what is meant by 'believing in God' has undergone a corresponding shift. And this, indeed, is what has happened; hence my heading for the final section of this chapter: 'The Changing Nature of Belief in God'.

'I believe in God.' Every Christian says this, or something like it, every time they perform that act of worship which is the credal confession of our Christian faith. What does it mean? This time, let's start at the modern end. Consider these three statements of belief: 'I believe in unicorns'; 'I believe in keeping out of debt'; 'I believe in Tony Blair'. Someone using the first of these expressions is almost certainly expressing the opinion that there are, in the real world, actual members of the class of unicorns. Most people don't say 'I believe in gods', but many people, even these days, *do* say: 'I believe in God'. And I suppose that, in saying this, many of them are saying something like: 'I believe that God exists', that God is as real as, or infinitely more real than, the other realities that there are. I can't imagine someone saying 'I believe in unicorn', in the singular. Perhaps we say 'I believe in God', in the singular, because debate, these days, rages not between those who believe in many gods and those who believe in one, but between those who believe that there is one real god and those who believe that all gods are fictional. The trouble is, of course, that, along this track, it is very difficult to avoid falling into the trap of supposing, as I put it earlier, that 'god' is the name of a particular kind of thing: namely, divine things. But, if this *is* how the statement is understood, then, for reasons that I indicated earlier, far from being an expression of Christian believing, such as might find its place at the outset of a Christian creed, it is incompatible with Christian (and Jewish, and Islamic) faith – because particular kinds of things, whether the kinds have one or many members, are what creatures are, jostling and competing with each other for space, and interest, and survival.

Let's try my second candidate: 'I believe in keeping out of debt'. Unlike 'I believe in unicorns', this is not an opinion as to a matter of fact, but rather an evaluation; its object is a policy of action, a way of living: keeping out of debt is what I ought to do. Facts and values, what 'is' the case and what we 'ought' to do, are so inextricably intertwined that sometimes, I suspect, when people say that they believe in God, they are expressing their commitment to a whole range of moral policies and attitudes which they take to be entailed by such belief. Nevertheless, the statement 'I believe in God', even taken as a declaration of ethical policy, is still not a Christian confession of faith.

It might seem obvious that 'I believe in Tony Blair' is the *least* plausible candidate to be considered by analogy with 'I believe in God'. It does, however, have something going for it. Whereas 'I believe in unicorns' merely expresses an opinion as to fact, and 'I believe in keeping out of debt' goes one step further by committing the speaker to a way of living, 'I believe in Tony Blair' takes us into quite different territory. It expresses the speaker's trust, whether prudently or imprudently, in someone else. It thereby brings us out of the isolated world of individual opinion and preference and evaluation into the realm of *relationships*, about which I shall have more to say in the following chapter.

These puzzles about 'believing' have a very ancient history. Way back in the fifth century, Saint Augustine gave them classical expression in distinguishing between three Latin constructions. '*Credere Deo*', he tells us, is believing in God in the sense of believing God, believing what God says. '*Credere Deum*' is a matter of believing God to be God, both in the sense of acknowledging that God exists and in the sense of acknowledging that the one we mention when we speak of 'God' is, as it were, the only *real* God. (The natural rendering of this, in English, would probably be 'believing in God' in the sense that, I have suggested, has become so problematic.) Finally, there is '*Credere* in *Deum*', the expression as we have it in the creeds; an expression with a sense of *movement*, of direction, of going somewhere, of 'godwardness', believing 'into' God. Here is Augustine's account: 'What is it, therefore, to believe in Him [*credere in eum*]? It is in believing to love, in believing to delight, in believing to walk towards him, and be incorporated amongst the limbs or members of his body.'[16]

We live in a culture in which many people, believers and nonbelievers alike, seem to think that the word 'god' is really quite easy to use. We have developed a dangerous kind of deafness to the wisdom of all the world's great religious traditions – Christianity, Judaism, Islam, Upanishadic Hinduism, perhaps also some strands of Buddhism – which, having learned the hard way, have for centuries insisted that speaking appropriately of God is, while not impossible, the most difficult, the most demanding, the most dangerous thing that human speech can do, because appropriate speech brings to language appropriate relationship. But, if this is the case, and if the word 'God' (with a capital 'G') has today become so burdened with inappropriate use, why don't we simply discard it, and speak in some other way about the holy mystery which the word misnames? After all, it is not on a three-letter word that our hearts, identities and hopes are set. The short answer, I suggest, is that the long, and complex, and conflictual history of humankind's engagement in the educational process of learning non-idolatrously to worship, learning wholeheartedly and without reserve to give ourselves to the truth, and flourishing, and freedom, to which we have been called, is simply too bound up with the history of the uses and misuses of this little word. However difficult it is to use appropriately, there is no *other* word which similarly signals that the truth and destiny and healing of the world infinitely outstrip the world's capacities.

Notes

1   Salley Vickers, *Miss Garnet's Angel* (London: HarperCollins, 2001), pp. 327–328.
2   John Henry Newman, *The Letters and Diaries of John Henry Newman. Vol. XXX*, edited by Charles Stephen Dessain and Thomas Gornall, S. J. (Oxford: Clarendon Press, 1976), pp. 159–160.
3   The previous two paragraphs are largely taken from Nicholas Lash, 'On Learning to be Wise', *Priests and People* (October 2001), pp. 355–359; p. 356.
4   Cf. Lash, 'On Learning to be Wise', p. 359.
5   Daniel 13: 43.
6   See, for example, the closing pages of Stephen W. Hawking, *A Brief History of Time* (London: Bantam Press, 1988).
7   See Michael J. Buckley, *At the Origins of Modern Atheism* (New Haven and London: Yale University Press, 1987).
8   Cf. Julius Lipner, *The Hindus. Their Religious Beliefs and Practices* (London: Routledge, 1994), p. 305; discussed by me in Nicholas Lash, *The Beginning and the End of 'Religion'* (Cambridge: Cambridge University Press, 1996), p. 52.
9   See Lash, *Beginning and End of 'Religion'*, pp. 22–23.
10   See Exodus 3: 13–14.
11   The subversive implications of this have been beautifully indicated in a comment on the Five Ways by Denys

Turner: 'in showing God to exist reason shows that we no longer know what "exists" means' (Denys Turner, 'On Denying the Right God: Aquinas on Atheism and Idolatry', *Modern Theology*, Vol. 20, No. 1 (January 2004), pp. 141–61; p. 158).

12   See James M. Byrne, *God* (London: Continuum, 2001), p. 69 and elsewhere; and my review in *The Tablet* (15 September 2001), p. 1300.

13   Alert readers may wonder whether there are not things that may be said of God not metaphorically but analogically. Although it would take another essay to furnish warrants for the assertion, I believe that modern uses of the concept of 'metaphor' are capacious enough to take account of thirteenth-century distinctions between metaphorical and analogical predication.

14   Fergus Kerr, *After Aquinas. Versions of Thomism* (London: Blackwell, 2002), p. 187.

15   John Henry Newman, *The Theological Papers of John Henry Newman on Faith and Certainty*, partly prepared for publication by Hugo M. de Achaval, S. J.; selected and edited by J. Derek Holmes; with a note of introduction by Charles Stephen Dessain (Oxford: Clarendon Press, 1976), p. 102.

16   Augustine's discussion may be found in his *Commentary on John,* xxix (*PL*, 35, 1631). The somewhat free translation is my own: see Nicholas Lash, *Believing Three Ways in One God* (London: SCM Press Ltd, 1992; Notre Dame: University of Notre Dame Press, 1993; London: SCM Press Ltd, 2002, with a Preface by Laurence P. Hemming), p. 20.

Chapter 2

Globalization and Holiness

'Only One Earth'

As I remarked in the previous chapter, it is not easy to think Christian thoughts in a culture whose imagination, whose ways of 'seeing' the world and everything there is to see, are increasingly unschooled by Christianity and, to an alarming extent, quite hostile to it. The situation in which we find ourselves is, I have suggested, one in which, if Christians wish to retain the use of the word 'God', they will undoubtedly be misunderstood, because the word has now come to be the name of the members of a class of actual or possible things or entities of a particular kind, a kind that some people call 'divine' and others (displaying their ignorance of the history of the word) 'supernatural'.[1]

If this is what 'gods' have now become, then, as already mentioned, orthodox Christians, Jews and Muslims share with atheists a *dis*belief in gods, for none of them believe such things exist. (And the fact that this way of putting the matter will probably puzzle many readers is an indication of the depth of our predicament.) If, on the other hand, Christians were to discard the troublesome little word 'god' from their vocabulary, they would render unintelligible the narratives which give them their identity, cutting themselves off from the long and complex history of the uses and misuses of the word, a history which may, nevertheless, contain irreplaceable clues, of inestimable importance, as to the way the world goes and as to our place and destiny, within that world, as human beings.

For most of its history, the word 'god' and its cognates have named the term of a *relationship*: the relationship of worshipping. Everybody worships something – has their heart set somewhere – and what you worship is your god or gods. Worship may take many forms, from the reverence and respect we pay to those whom we admire to the (arguably unachievable) total and absolute surrender of the self to the holy mystery whose generosity all things express by their existence. In this connection, I suggested that the great religious traditions of the world may best be understood as *schools* in which people learn thus to worship while thereby learning *not* to worship any 'thing': any fact or feature of the world; not themselves, not their nation, nor its leader; not any story, value, dream, ideal or memory.

I propose, in this chapter, to reflect on those aspects of our experience, as human beings, in relation to which the Christian tradition came to 'name' the incomprehensible mystery of God as 'Holy Spirit'. After some remarks about 'globalization' and about what I call 'the recovery of grand narrative', I shall – under the headings of 'Renewing the Spirit' and 'Renewing Religion' – recommend the recovery of a sense of 'spirit' as vitality bestowed, life given, and of 'religion' as the symbolization of social identity. The chapter will conclude with some observations on 'holiness and sacramentality'.

In 1972, Barbara Ward and René Dubos published a report, commissioned by the United Nations, entitled *Only One Earth: The Care and Maintenance of a Small Planet*. On the cover was one of those astonishing images of the earth photographed from space. For the first time, human beings could take in at a glance the singleness and beauty of their home.[2]

The three decades since that report appeared have seen a deepening and unprecedented recognition of the global interconnectedness of every fact, event and circumstance; of wealth and poverty, success and failure, life and death. 'We all make up one world,' says Nicholas Boyle, 'even if we are only gradually coming to recognize it.'[3]

'No man is an island,' said John Donne, four hundred years ago, 'every man is a piece of the continent, a part of the main.'[4] And yet, the scientific world view emerging in Donne's day was one which saw the fundamental constituents of reality as minute particles, individuals, in emptiness. Today, even in physics, the atomic individual entity has been dethroned and, guided by so-called 'chaos theory' (which is not, of course, about chaos at all, but about the unpredictable order of the world), 'every schoolchild knows' that rainfall in Topeka, Kansas, may follow from the flapping of a butterfly's wings in Tokyo. We have begun to learn, again, the interconnectedness of everything, the primacy of *relations*.

The buzzword these days, of course, is 'globalization'. During the twentieth century, the world became, for the first time, a single economic fact, a single global network of forces of production, distribution and exchange: a global market. And while that market, as at present structured, makes a minority of mankind immensely rich, it deepens the destructive poverty of many millions more.[5]

Here are a handful of chilling statistics. 'In the USA ten years ago the income of company directors was 42 times higher than that of blue-collar workers; it is now 419 times higher ... Among 4.5 billion residents of "developing" countries ... a third have no access to drinkable water ... and a fifth have no use of sanitary and medical services ... In 70–80 of the 100 or so "developing" countries the average income per head of the population is today lower than ten or even 30 years ago. At the same time, three of the richest men in the world have private assets greater than the combined national product of the 48 poorest countries', while the 500 richest people on Earth own more than the entire gross domestic product of Africa.[6]

'One thing', however, 'which has thus far escaped globalization is our collective ability to act globally.'[7] In other words, the most urgent challenge that confronts the human race today is the requirement to imagine and to construct a global *politics* which can contain and counter the destructive violence unleashed by the unchecked operation of a global market that is at present structured to work in the interests of a handful of the richest and most powerful institutions and individuals in the world. What shape such a politics will take, we do not know. We have not been here before. Perhaps the first beginnings may be glimpsed in the history of the United Nations (for all its weakness and fragility) and in the development of international law and instruments of international justice.[8] One thing we can be sure of: it will not take the form of a 'world state'. Why not? Because the state is that institution on behalf of which the citizen is called to patriotic duty and, to put it very simply, it makes no sense to talk about a patriotic duty to the *planet,* because the planet has no political opponents.[9] It seems to me, however, that at least as important as the construction of appropriate institutions will be the development of what one might call a genuinely global *imagination*; a sense of solidarity with the whole of humankind – past, present and future.

We all learn who 'we' are, develop a sense of identity, of the relationships which make us *us*, in some particular place, at some particular time. We are the children of *these* parents, have these brothers and sisters, friends and enemies and neighbours. If all goes well, however, we gradually learn a more far-reaching loyalty than that to our immediate family, village, tribe: we discover ourselves entangled in relationships of language, culture, trade, with innumerable other people, most of whom we shall never meet or know by name, but for whose well-being we learn that we must bear some measure of responsibility. The way the world now is, it makes no sense whatsoever to suppose that 'political' education in this general sense, as education in social relationships and responsibilities, should cease when it reaches the boundaries of the nation-state. 'Globalization' requires us now to learn that who 'we' are is nothing less than everyone.

In the development of such a genuinely global imagination, Christianity undoubtedly has a part to play. (That is a positive assertion with no negative implications: many other traditions – political, philosophical, cultural and religious – indubitably have their parts to play as well.) Christianity has a part to play not simply because it has been around for a long time and continues to shape the identity of very many people (one-sixth of the population of the planet, for example, is at present at least nominally Roman Catholic), but also on account of its own self-constituting narrative, or what we usually call the doctrine of the Church.

I will spell this out, at this point, very briefly, because it raises issues to which I shall return. 'Church', *'ecclesia'*, means gathering, assembly, congregation; a people summoned, called together for some task. This people is the human race: called, out of nothing, into common life, communion, in God. This does not make all human beings Christians. What we usually *call* 'Church' is that *particular* people which thus announces, symbolizes, dramatizes the fact and possibility and promise of the common peoplehood, exceptionless communion, of the whole of humankind. (The notorious slogan 'outside the Church there is no salvation' has always had two senses: that only Christians may be saved is false; that salvation is the healing of relations, the gathering of humankind into *'ecclesia'*, communion, in God, is true. Bishop

Christopher Butler was fond of quoting the Orthodox theologian Paul Evdokimov: 'We know where the Church is; it is not for us to judge and say where the Church is not.'[10])

The Recovery of Grand Narrative

We all learn who 'we' are, we acquire and develop a sense of identity, of the relationships which make us *us*, in some particular place, at some particular time. And we articulate our identity in narrative. I was born in India, where my father was in the army. That does not tell the reader much, but even so brief a story tells the reader *something* about who I am.

Autobiography is particular: my story will not be identical to yours. Most of the stories that we tell, however, begin with 'we', embrace a larger group than merely the narrator. But can we tell a story in which 'we' refers to everyone, living and dead and as yet unborn; to all of humankind and the entire context of creation in which human lives are lived? Can we, in other words, tell true stories of the world? There seem, these days, to be as many varieties of 'postmodernism' as there are postmodernists, but one thing upon which all of them agree is that the day of 'grand narratives', of stories of everything, is ended. There simply is, they say, no *single* 'real world' of which a true and total story could be told. It is, however, 'really rather extraordinary', as Nicholas Boyle points out, 'that the belief that there is "no single world" for us to have knowledge of ... should have gained such ground at a time when the unity and boundedness of our planetary existence has become more ... visible, than at any previous time in the history of the human race'.[11]

The discernible oneness of the world, of the interconnectedness of everything, not only makes the telling of some story of the world, some story of the *whole* world, a possibility: it makes it a necessity. Globalization requires us to try to tell a story in which 'the world' refers to everything, and in which 'we' refers to the whole of humankind. Any such suggestion still often meets with stiff resistance, two of the most widespread and influential forms of which we could call the 'narrative is fiction' and the 'grand narratives are imperialist' objections.

'Narrative is Fiction'

The suspicion that story-tellers spin false fables, and that truth is therefore to be sought elsewhere than in narrative, goes back at least as far as Plato. However, it took its most powerful hold on Western culture in the seventeenth and eighteenth centuries. The culture of Enlightenment sought explanation of everything, through measurement and rigorous description, from nowhere in particular. It was a culture which suspected the complexity of metaphor, the open-endedness of narrative; a culture which, in quest of certainty, feared the fragility of particulars and contingencies. The slogan that best captured this mentality was Lessing's pronouncement, in 1777, that 'Accidental truths of history can never become the proof of a necessary truth of reason'.[12]

Over a hundred years before, Descartes and Galileo and their contemporaries had excluded the human mind from 'the subject-matter of science'.[13] This separation of consciousness from nature,[14] of speech and thought from what we speak and think about, sustained the illusion that human beings can speak the truth from nowhere in particular, that 'reason' springs from no particular soil.[15]

Ironically, Lessing's 'ugly ditch' between the 'accidental truths of history' and the 'necessary truths of reason', between narrative and explanation, turned out to be a figment of the modern imagination, because the truths of reason are never quite as necessary as those who formulate them may suppose, and we cannot exclude the possibility that historical contingency may bear the meaning of the world and, perhaps, the truth of God.

The world is 'story-shaped'. True stories, however, are always difficult to tell, not merely because our understanding is so limited, but because our capacity for self-delusion appears to be unbounded. The narratives of every tribe, and class, and nation are distorted by ignorance, and arrogance, and fear. The achievement of a genuinely global imagination, a sense of solidarity with the whole of humankind, is a breathtakingly daunting ambition. Nevertheless, if the 'narrative is fiction' objection boils down to little more than a reminder of the difficulty of telling, truthfully, stories that are true, it is hardly an insuperable barrier, in principle, to the elaboration of some true 'story of the world'.

'Grand Narratives are Imperialist'

I turn next to the objection that grand narratives are imperialist. It is undoubtedly the case that they frequently have been and that many of them are vulnerable to imperial ambition. Here is John L. O'Sullivan, the man who came up with the notion of 'manifest destiny', writing in 1839:

> All this will be our future history, to establish on earth the moral dignity and salvation of man – the immutable truth and beneficence of God. For this blessed mission to the nations of the world, which are shut out from the life-giving light of truth, has America been chosen; and her high example shall smite unto death the tyranny of kings, hierarchs, and oligarchs, and carry the glad tidings of peace and good will where myriads now endure an existence scarcely more enviable than that of beasts of the field. Who, then, can doubt that our country is destined to be *the great nation* of futurity?[16]

The battlefields and other graveyards of the world bear witness to the frequency with which imperial oppression has been fuelled by one form or another of the dangerous and destructive fantasy of 'manifest destiny', of the illusion that 'we' alone have truth, and providence, and God, upon our side, and that we are therefore entitled to impose our values and our views on everybody else.

The charge that grand narratives are imperialist by their very nature presumes, however, that there can only be one true 'story of everything'. But all stories are selective, weaving particular patterns of interpretation. No story says everything, not even a story of everything! All stories have an angle, a perspective, a point of view. And in order to test the truth of a story, it is necessary to understand the point of view from which it is told.

This is not an argument for what one might call metaphysical relativism. Stories of everything may indeed be mutually exclusive, either in respect of particular features or of the overall account they try to render of the way things are. Nevertheless, establishing the respects in which, and the extent to which, differences amount to disagreements and disagreement, in turn, signals contradiction, is an undertaking which demands of the participants sustained attentiveness and respect, and a willingness to acquire new ways of thought, fresh habits of imagination.

I am suggesting, in other words, that far from grand narrative being imperialist in *principle*, the expectation should be that the truth of a story of everything will be enriched and deepened through engagement with those who tell a different story. To put it as simply as possible: truth is a gift, never a possession or commodity, and it is *as* a gift that it should be shared. (There are, I believe, very good reasons for treating the current preoccupation with 'intellectual property rights' with moral as well as intellectual suspicion.)

For all the vast diversity of languages, and cultures, and traditions in the world, there does not seem to be, in fact, a limitless variety of types of grand narrative. At least as a provisional and broad-brush generalization, we might suggest that they appear to be reducible to *four*.

On the one hand, there are *materialisms* of the kind described by the philosopher Antony Flew as announcing that 'all there is is, in the last analysis, stuff; and that whatever is not stuff is nonsense'.[17] (Whether such stories can be told coherently is an interesting question: does Professor Richard Dawkins, who purports to be a materialist of this kind, *really* believe that his freedom to decide what tale to tell is quite illusory?)

On the other hand, there are *idealisms* which would persuade us that the world of our experience is woven out of dreams, ideas, illusion – and that if there is more to everything than the outcomes of the mind's construction, no human mind could ever know it. There are disciplined and noble versions of idealism, and there are versions as degenerate as the nonsense talked by those who suppose that this, that or the other may be 'true for me'.

For both these first two types, the story of the world is a story without plot or purpose: things simply *are* the way they are, or seem to be. William James expressed a feeling widespread under the impact of Darwinism when he wrote: 'It is impossible, in the present temper of the scientific imagination, to find in the drifting of the cosmic atoms ... anything but a kind of aimless weather, doing and undoing, achieving no proper history, and leaving no result.'[18] In the third place, however, there are darker tales than any told by James, according to which the purpose of the world is power: strength conquers weakness, and it is violence which makes the world go round. Nietzsche's greatness as a philosopher consists not simply in the skill with which he tells this story, but in his prophetic ability to make us recognize how frighteningly *plausible* it is. I confess that I have much more sympathy with those who are haunted by the terrifying possibility that such a story may be true than I do with the idiots who go round telling us that everything is not only good but permanently getting better.

Finally, there are counterfactual narratives which do not so much *contradict* the nihilist's despairing story (as optimism does, as tales of 'progress' do) as subvert it, announcing that, notwithstanding the darkness and the terror of the world, the prevalence of pain and suffering, nevertheless the first word and the last is *peace*: that all there is is not 'brute fact' but *gift*, gift given in tranquillity, and that the ending of all things is peace. It is no coincidence that the nearest to a 'proper name' that Thomas Aquinas could come up with for the third way Christians confess the holy mystery of God to be was 'gift'. To understand all things as given, as expression of the giving that is God's own self, and the outcome of all giving to be life and harmony, is to understand what Christians mean by 'Holy Spirit'. That, at least, is the suggestion that I now wish to explore.

Renewing the Spirit

When people talk, these days, of 'spirits', if they don't mean vodka, they usually mean ghosts. Most people do not believe in ghosts but, increasingly, they hold in very high esteem things 'spiritual' and 'spirituality'. In fact, amongst the chattering classes, 'spirituality' is far more highly regarded than 'religion', because 'religion' is entangled in the public realm of ritual and behaviour, of institutions and beliefs, a realm in which questions about truth and duty may be raised, whereas the 'spiritual' floats free from fact and calculation and responsibility, massaging in fantasies of feeling the bruised narcissism of well-heeled individualists.

My German dictionary offers, as translations of '*Geist*': 'spirit', 'mind', 'genius', 'brains', 'intellect', 'cleverness', 'spectre', 'ghost'. The German distinction between '*Geist*' and '*Natur*', or 'nature', has roughly corresponded to the distinction, in English, between 'mind' and 'matter'. What is so disturbing about contemporary interest in the 'spiritual' is that now, not merely matter, but mind *as well*, is being excluded from its territory: if someone says that they are fascinated by things 'spiritual', they are most unlikely to be expressing an interest in (to quote the dictionary again) 'genius', 'brains', 'intellect' or 'cleverness'. In such a situation, any attempt to speak sensibly of *God* as 'spirit' must first take the long road through an effort to recapture a less distorted understanding of what being *human* means.

Discussion about how 'consciousness' is best understood is at present a very lively field in a wide range of scientific disciplines and in philosophy. Are 'mind' and 'matter', for example, best understood as different kinds of thing, as different entities? Those who answer 'Yes' are known as 'substance dualists', because they think of mind and matter as two substances, or things. Unfortunately, most scientists and many philosophers are poor historians, thus perpetuating by assertion the widespread but quite mistaken belief that traditional Christianity is committed to some form of substance dualism. In a conference in which he and I took part a few years ago, I took issue with the philosopher John Searle for referring to 'traditional dualism, the belief in the immortality of the soul, spiritualism, and so on'.[19]

Where mind and matter are concerned, I pointed out that, in the tradition going back to Aristotle, 'mind' might be best defined as 'the capacity for behaviour of the complicated and symbolic kinds which constitute the linguistic, social, moral, economic, scientific, cultural, and other characteristic activities of human beings in society'.[20]

Think of your mind, then, not as a 'thing', stuck somewhere in your head, but as your *ability* to do the kinds of things that human beings, distinctively and characteristically, do: they make plans, tell stories, dream dreams, and construct elaborate systems of organization and behaviour. And then try to think in a similar way about the distinction between the 'body' and the 'soul'. In a similar way, but not identically. The distinction is similar because to speak of ourselves as 'souls' is, like talk of 'minds', to speak of our ability to do the kinds of things that human beings, distinctively and characteristically, do. However, talk of 'minds' stops there, whereas to talk of ourselves as 'souls' is (if what we say is to be within earshot of classical Christianity) to go further. To speak of ourselves as 'souls' is to recognize our creatureliness, to acknowledge that everything we are and have is *gift*; that we are 'gift-things' that have been given the capacity and duty to return the gift we are in praise and celebration.

There is a quite straightforward distinction between, for example, a pineapple and its shape. But nobody supposes that its 'shape' is a second, different kind of thing, somewhere inside (or perhaps on the surface of) the pineapple! Think of the soul as the 'shape' of a human life: the body's history, identity, direction – and, we hope, its destiny in God.

As well as the distinction between 'mind' and 'matter', and the distinction between 'soul' and 'body', there is another distinction, familiar to every reader of the Scriptures, between 'spirit' and 'flesh'. To recover some sense of the way in which this distinction works, however, we have to get back behind not only the 'substance dualisms' of modernity, but also behind all forms of the distinction between the body and the soul. The biblical distinction is not between living systems and their capacities (as distinctions between mind and matter, souls and bodies, are) but between things coming alive, and things crumbling into dust; between not-life, or life-gone-wrong, and life: true life, real life, God's life and all creation's life in God. The central metaphor is that of wind, the breath of life, the breath God is and breathes. Whether, sent forth from God, breathing all creatures into being, renewing the Earth and filling it with good things; whether whispering gently to Elijah, or making 'the oaks to whirl, and [stripping] the forests bare'; or breathing peace on the disciples for the forgiveness of sins – it is one wind, one spirit, which 'blows where it wills' and we do not know where it comes from or where it goes.[21] To confess God as Spirit is to tell the story of the world as something, from its beginning to its end, given to come alive.[22]

This seems a good point at which to pick up a suggestion that I made in passing in the previous chapter: the suggestion that there are at least some contexts in which it might make more sense to regard the word 'God' as a verb rather than a noun. When considering this possibility, Aquinas calls in evidence the eighth-century Greek theologian John of Damascus, according to whom the Greek word '*theos*' (the cognates of which would be '*deus*' in Latin, 'god' or 'deity' in English) 'functions more like a verb than a noun, as if it designated not a being but a doing'.[23] And although Aquinas decided that, on balance, the 'agent' that God is may not be so understood as simply to collapse the agent into agency, being into doing, nevertheless Fergus Kerr is able to say, in summary: 'Thomas's God, anyway, is more like an event than an entity.'[24] In the present context, then, my suggestion is that to speak of God as 'Spirit' is not to say that God is one of the kinds of thing that 'spirits' are (whatever that may be), because God is not a thing of *any* kind. It is, rather, to confess God as inexhaustible generosity, limitless donation: '*Dominum et vivificantem*'.[25] (That phrase in the Creed is usually rendered as 'Lord and lifegiver', though 'lording and lifegiving' might be a more accurate translation.)

The philosopher Mary Midgley has said that 'Gaia – the idea of life on earth as a self-sustaining natural system – is a central concept for our age'.[26] She is surely correct. It makes sense, I suggest, to see, in 'Green' movements, the reawakening of a dimension of the Christian story of the world which had been almost lost sight of in mainstream modern Christianity. Unsurprisingly, when uncorrected by *other* dimensions of the story – by the insistence, for example, on the absolute transcendence of One who cannot be 'mapped' onto any of the systems of the world – it loses its way, mistaking the gift that Gaia is for the giver, mistaking the creature that is the living system of the world for that world's creator. Christianity is not pantheism, and Gaia is not God.

Renewing Religion

Having said something about 'spirit', it is now time for some remarks on 'holiness', for God, in Christianity, is confessed as 'Holy Spirit'.

Holiness is not primarily a *moral* quality, as truthfulness or kindness are. There are, after all, not only holy people, but also holy times and holy places. Etymologically, the 'holy' is the whole, the healed. To make holiness an attribute of God is to acknowledge, in the object of our worship, all the fullness, the completeness, the wholeness which we lack. Only in a purely derivative sense may creatures be called holy, and we call those people, times and places 'holy' in which we recognize that we are drawing near to God.

The holy, in its fullness, lies outside our control. In the presence of the holy, you take off your shoes and silence the clamour of self-interest. The holy is defined in contrast to the profane, to whatever is *pro-fanum*, lies before, outside, the temple. This is the same distinction as that drawn between the 'secular' and the 'sacred'. 'Sacred' times and places, things and people, are those that we do not control. The sacred, you might say, is that which is too hot to handle.

It will have been noticed that, so far, no mention has been made of 'religion'. It is now time to make good that omission. Hegel defined religion as 'the point where a nation defines for itself what it regards as truth'.[27] Nicholas Boyle glosses that definition as follows: 'A culture's religion expresses what the people of that culture ... *really take seriously*.'[28] That comes quite close, I think, to my description of the sacred as that which is too hot to handle.

In the previous chapter, defining 'gods' as whatever people worship, whatever it is on which their hearts are set, I said that I can only find out what you worship, what your gods are, by asking you and by observing your behaviour. And I added that, of course, these days, most people do not *name* as 'gods' the gods they worship. The same is true of religious beliefs and practices, of what people treat as sacred. Whatever a social group takes really seriously, finds too hot to handle, believes to be beyond control, is the territory marked out, in that society, as sacred; is the character of its religion.

The fact that, under the influence of Enlightenment hostility to Christianity, most people now use the word 'religion' very differently, is neither here nor there. People's behaviour is a better guide to their convictions than the terminology they use. When Margaret

Thatcher declared: 'You can't buck the market', she was confessing that, in her scheme of things, the market was deemed sacred, outside even her control.

In the previous chapter, I quoted a letter in which Newman said that 'men of the world do not see' what he called the 'special and primary office of religion', seeing only 'its poverty as a principle of secular progress'. I did not then mention what Newman, in that letter, takes that 'office of religion' to be. For what he calls 'Christianity in its social aspect', this 'special and primary office of religion' is, he tells us, 'being the binding principle of society'.[29] That sounds to me not only quite like Hegel, fifty years earlier, but also quite like Émile Durkheim, twenty years later when, in his study of *Suicide*, the great sociologist defined religion as 'the system of symbols by means of which society becomes conscious of itself; it is the characteristic way of thinking of collective existence'.[30]

In the United States, the flag is a religious symbol, a key expression of the religion that is American nationalism. The flag is sacred. In England, by contrast, uncertainty about exactly who we are, and how to tell our story, is reflected in the confusion as to what might count, in *this* society, as giving symbolic expression to its identity. John Major had a go with ladies bicycling to evensong, but that did not quite work.

Most religion is, of course, idolatrous. We ascribe divinity to, we treat as sacred, a vast diversity of ideas and institutions, people, places, stories, customs, which are, at worst, destructive of ourselves and of the world in which we live and, at best, ambivalent intimations of where true holiness, beyond all our construction and imagination, might be found.

Thus it is that the great religious traditions of the world function as *schools* in which people learn that there is no feature of the world – no nation, institution, person, text, idea, ambition – that is, quite simply, sacred. To be a pupil in these schools (and all the teachers in these schools are pupils too) is to learn that we are called *beyond* the worship of the creature; to learn that that which alone is truly 'holy' is quite beyond location and imagination, radically transcends the secular in which we live and die, bearing the gift and burden of contingent freedom. It is within the world, in *all* the world, in all we think and do and say and see, achieve and suffer, and by no means only in some small margin of the world which people, these days, call 'religion', that we are required to be attentive to the promptings of the Spirit, responsive to the breath of God.

Holiness and Sacramentality

It is a commonplace of theological journalism that the doctrine of the Holy Spirit has been neglected in Western theology. Where the story (at least since the Reformation) is concerned, it would seem more accurate to say, in the first place, that Protestantism's admirable recovery of focus and concentration on the *second* article of the Creed, on the doctrine of God's Word – enfleshed, proclaimed, inscribed – led, in the Protestant mainstream, to a relative neglect of the doctrines of Creation and the Spirit, the subject of the other two articles.[31] (When Schleiermacher, in the early nineteenth century, begins to recover a sense of the indwelling, uncreated Spirit, enlivening all things, he is suspect of pantheism – which may say more in criticism of the culture than of Schleiermacher! In England, this recovery took longer: in my study, I have the splendid edition of the works of Bishop Joseph Butler edited by William Gladstone – surely the theologically best educated of all British Prime Ministers. In the index, there is one entry under 'Grace'. It reads: 'Grace at meals recommended.'[32])

In the second place, Catholicism's counter-emphasis on the other two articles was, as it were, doubly deflected by the intellectual climate of modernity. Under pressure from modernity's obsession with proof, and certainty, and explanation, the doctrine of Creation was deflected into apologetic preoccupation with a newly invented enterprise known as 'natural theology', the search for 'proofs' that God exists, while the imaginative framework in which the doctrine of the Spirit's work, in church and sacraments, was treated, shifted from the language of drama, and metaphor, and symbol, to that of the structure and duties of an institution.

I have argued for many years that the key *doctrinal* achievement of the second Vatican Council is to be seen in the sequence of chapters of its two Dogmatic Constitutions, on Revelation and on the Church. Where the latter is concerned, an opening chapter on the irreducible *diversity* of images and metaphors that is required if we are to think appropriately about the mystery of God's gathering of humankind is followed by a chapter which nevertheless gives relative pride of place to *one* of these images: that of the Church as a *people*, a people drawn through time to God. Only then, in a third chapter, does the Constitution consider the kinds of structures and offices which such a people needs.

The first article of the Constitution describes the Church, 'By her relationship with Christ', as 'a kind of sacrament or sign of intimate union with God, and of the unity of all mankind', and the fourth article, in imagery as old as Ezechiel, speaks of the Church as the dwelling-place or temple of 'the Spirit of life, a fountain of water springing up to life eternal'.[33]

Historically, and sociologically, there is not, of course, the slightest doubt that the entire 'symbol system' that is Christianity – this vast and ancient network of stories and associations, of images and rituals and enactments, confused, argumentative, conflictual – is something that human beings have done, to both their glory and their shame.

However, the truth of this acknowledgement is not undermined by the deeper recognition that, in the last resort, everything we are and have is *gift*; that our best and truest speech is, not monologue but 'proslogue': address, response – to each other, and to the holy mystery which moves us to respond.

In a world so comprehensively disfigured by the accumulating consequences of our rapacity and unconcern and egotism, the 'giftness' of reality is, to put it mildly, not self-evident. Where might we look for hints and indications that, nevertheless, it is in some such terms that the story of the world is most truly and appropriately told?

A good place to start, perhaps, would be with the strange fact of forgiveness. Forgiveness, the restoration of relations, cannot be required by statute or achieved by force. And yet, with whatever fragility, however fitfully and incompletely, forgiveness does, in fact, occur – not merely between individuals but also, as the recent history of South Africa has shown, as a social reality. And forgiveness is pure gift, beyond all calculation, unamenable to causal explanation. And it was, of course, to the experience of forgiveness that the disciples of Jesus bore witness.

Closely related to forgiveness is what we might call the radicalization of the Golden Rule: 'In everything do to others as you would have them do to you.'[34] As an ethical maxim, the Rule is not, of course, peculiar to Christianity: 'it exists in Judaism, in Greek and Chinese culture and so on.'[35] In a passage entitled 'Relationship as holiness', the German theologian Christoph Theobald remarks that, on the surface, the Rule may be presented as 'a simple indication of the basic reciprocity which governs ... human relations'. And yet, however discreetly, it appeals to a capacity, which no law can require nor any violence achieve, to put oneself in someone else's place. To do so is pure gift and its full form, which we see on Calvary, is that of taking another's violence on oneself.

Here is Theobald again:

> When we realize that the future of the globe depends not only on a global justice which is in itself difficult to conceive, but on human figures and communities capable of living according to the truth of their consciences and exposing themselves to the violence of others without retaliating with the same weapons, we ... 'measure' the miraculous character of the effective and infinitely diversified emergence of these attitudes in our history.[36]

What Professor Theobald calls 'miraculous', I have called pure gift, beyond all explanation. (Readers will, I hope, by now agree that 'globalization' and 'holiness' have more to do with each other than they may have thought when they first came across the title of this chapter.)

The Christian story of everything, I have been suggesting, is the story of God's being as gift, as self-gift establishing and enlivening the world.[37] There are, of course, as many versions of this story as there are Christian theologies, ancient and modern. In recent decades, considerable emphasis has been laid, in Catholic Christianity, on what is called the 'preferential option for the poor'. The phrase was coined at the 1968 conference of Latin American episcopal conferences at Medellín in Colombia, which was convened to apply the teaching of the second Vatican Council to that continent. Reflecting on Medellín some twenty years later, Archbishop Marcos McGrath of Panama said that the Latin American Church was committed 'not only' to 'a preferential option for the poor in economic and political terms', but that this option was to be applied 'first of all to the evangelization of the poor, so that with them and from their point of view we can carry out the evangelization of the entire community'.[38]

In the present context, I am suggesting that to endorse the 'preferential option' is to tell and to perform the Christian story of the world, the story of the world as gift and action of God's liveliness, of Holy Spirit, 'with and from the point of view of' the victims of that same world's avarice, and violence, and power. It is ironic that whereas Gandhi, who was not a Christian, would have understood this story, few Christians in the well-fed West have yet begun to understand its implications. As the Dominican Herbert McCabe once put it: 'We for the most part shy off being human because if we are really human we will be crucified.'[39]

What does God look like? The Archangel Raphael, you will remember, suggested: 'courage and truth and mercy and right action'.[40] We can now be a little more specific. God looks like the action of the 'holy spirit' that God is said to be: like forgiveness and non-violence, solidarity with the victims, the achievement of communion in the one world to which all of us belong. This is not, of course, the end of the matter. There is also the question, at which I have just hinted, of the *cost* of holiness because, according to the Christian story of the world, God also looks like a young man, tortured, strung up on a Roman gibbet. The next question to be considered is: what does that death *say*?

Notes

1   Perhaps it might be helpful to say a word about that sideswipe against contemporary uses of the term 'supernatural'. Originally, the word was used adjectively or adverbially, to indicate the condition of creatures enabled, by God's grace, to act beyond the capacities of their given nature. As I have often pointed out to students, if you come across a rabbit playing Mozart on

the violin, you can bet your bottom dollar that that rabbit is acting supernaturally. Rabbits have not got it in them to play the violin. Moreover, things being the way they are with human sinfulness, if you come across human beings acting with consistent kindness, selflessness and generosity, the same assumption is in order. We simply have not got it in us to be that virtuous. On this account, it is possible that creatures, graced by God's enlivening gift, may act supernaturally. God, alone, cannot be supernatural, cannot act supernaturally, for what would graciously 'elevate' or heal *God's* 'nature'?

In time, unfortunately, people forgot all this and, having decided that all that there is in the familiar world, the world which we inhabit and explore, may be lumped together under the one word 'Nature' (which rapidly acquired the capital initial letter), they described those who supposed that, over and above this real world of nature, there are forces and entities of some other, higher order, as postulating the existence of 'supernatural' beings, the very head or chief of which is the being which religious believers know as 'god'.

In other words, this fundamental shift in usage of the concept of the supernatural (which shift, from the start, rendered religious belief suspect of superstition) was, albeit unintentionally, pregnant with atheism.

2 See Barbara Ward and René Dubos, *Only One Earth: The Care and Maintenance of a Small Planet* (New York and Harmondsworth: Penguin Books, 1972).

3 Nicholas Boyle, *Who Are We Now? Christian Humanism and the Global Market from Hegel to Heaney* (Edinburgh and Notre Dame: T. & T. Clark and the University of Notre Dame Press, 1998), p. 9.

4 John Donne, 'Devotions upon Emergent Occasions, *Meditation XVII'*, *The Major Works*, edited with an Introduction and Notes by John Carey (Oxford: Oxford University Press, 1990; Oxford World Classics, 2000), p. 344.

5 See Ian Linden, *A New Map of the World* (London: Darton, Longman and Todd, 2003).

6 Zygmunt Bauman, 'Whatever happened to compassion?', *The Moral Universe*, edited by Tom Bentley and Daniel Stedman Jones (London: Demos, 2001), pp. 51–56; p. 53; I take the final statistic from George Monbiot, 'The worst of times', *The Guardian*,

2 September 2003, p. 21. In Britain, at the beginning of 2003, 'the value of the companies in the FTSE-100 index had tumbled almost 50% from their peak three years earlier. Over the same period, however, boardroom pay advanced by more than 84%', while average earnings rose, in 2002, by 3% (*The Guardian*, 31 July 2003, p. 1).

7   Bauman, art. cit., p. 52.

8   According to Stefano Zamagni, Professor of Political Economy at the University of Bologna: 'The way to respond to the challenges of globalisation ... is through a transnational civil society, to be constructed with patience and determination' (Stefano Zamagni, *Economics, Conscience and Globalisation* [an 'occasional paper' published, in 2003, by the Maltese research institute Discern], p. 33). For an outstandingly fresh, well-informed and provocative discussion of the issues attending globalization, see Linden, *A New Map of the World*. Ian Linden was for many years Director of the Catholic Institute for International Relations.

9   See Boyle, *Who Are We Now?*, pp. 175–176.

10   Paul Evdokimov, *Orthodoxy*, cited by Christopher Butler, *The Theology of Vatican II. The Sarum Lectures 1966* (London: Darton, Longman and Todd, 1967), p. 133. Cf. Nicholas Lash, *Believing Three Ways in One God*, pp. 86–88.

11   Boyle, *Who Are We Now?*, p. 151.

12   G. E. Lessing, 'On the proof of the spirit and of power', *Lessing's Theological Writings*, selected and introduced by Henry Chadwick (London: Adam and Charles Black, 1956), p. 53.

13   John Searle, *The Rediscovery of the Mind* (London: MIT Press, 1992), p. 85.

14   See Stephen Toulmin, *Cosmopolis. The Hidden Agenda of Modernity* (Chicago: University of Chicago Press, 1990), p. 147.

15   See Nicholas Lash, 'Recovering Contingency', *Consciousness and Human Identity*, edited by John Cornwell (Oxford: Oxford University Press, 1990), p. 204.

16   John L. O'Sullivan, 'The Great Nation of Futurity', *Democratic Review* (1839), his stress.

17   A. Flew, *An Introduction to Western Philosophy: Ideas and Argument from Plato to Sartre* (London: Thames and Hudson, 1971), p. 45.

18 William James, *The Varieties of Religious Experience* (New York: Mentor Books, 1958), p. 407.

19 John Searle, *The Rediscovery of the Mind*, p. 3; discussed in Nicholas Lash, 'Recovering Contingency', p. 199.

20 Anthony Kenny, *The Metaphysics of Mind* (Oxford: Clarendon Press, 1989), p. 7; cited Lash, loc. cit.

21 See Psalm 104: 27, 29–30; 1 Kings 19: 12; Psalm 29: 9; John 20: 22–23; John 3: 8.

22 Cf. Lash, *Believing Three Ways*, p. 85.

23 Kerr, *After Aquinas*, p. 187.

24 Ibid., p. 190.

25 I am trying, in this small book, to sketch the Christian doctrine of God, the doctrine of God's Trinity, without undue technicality and in the context of some of the principal preoccupations of the world in which we live. It is, however, important to notice that Aquinas's attempt to sustain the tension between understanding the word 'God' as *substantival* or as *verbal* is grounded in his knowledge that whereas, where creatures are concerned, it is always possible to distinguish between their identity, on the one hand, and the roles and relationships into which they enter, on the other, no such distinction is applicable to God. The holy mystery of God simply *is* the acts or relations that God is said to be and do. Thus the Franciscan theologian Thomas Weinandy can say: 'Put succinctly and boldly, the persons of the Trinity are not nouns; they are verbs and the names which designate them – Father, Son and Holy Spirit – designate the acts by which they are defined' (Thomas G. Weinandy, *Does God Suffer?* [Notre Dame: University of Notre Dame Press, 2000], pp. 45–46; cited in Kerr, *After Aquinas*, p. 240).

26 Mary Midgley, 'Individualism and the Concept of Gaia', *The Moral Universe*, pp. 93–98; p. 93.

27 G.W.F. Hegel, *Vorlesungen über die Philosophie der Geschichte* (Frankfurt, 1970), p. 70; cited by Nicholas Boyle, *Who Are We Now?*, p. 85.

28 Boyle, loc. cit., my stress.

29 Newman, *Letters and Diaries, XXX*, p. 159.

30 Émile Durkheim, *Suicide. A Study in Sociology*, translated by John Spaulding and George Simpson (London: Routledge and Kegan Paul, 1952), p. 312.

31 It is no coincidence that the first volume of Karl Barth's *Church Dogmatics* should be devoted to *The Doctrine of*

the Word of God, whose 'threefold form' as 'revealed, written and proclaimed' (*Church Dogmatics. Vol. IV. The Doctrine of Reconciliation, 3/1,* translated by G. W. Bromiley [Edinburgh: T. & T. Clark, 1961], p. 114) he expounded at some length: see Barth, 'The Word of God in its Threefold Form', *Church Dogmatics. Vol. I. The Doctrine of the Word of God, I,* translated by G. T. Thomson (Edinburgh: T. & T. Clark, 1936), pp. 98–140.

32   *The Works of Joseph Butler, D. C. L.,* edited by W. E. Gladstone, *Volume II* (Oxford: Clarendon Press, 1896), p. 454.

33   Second Vatican Council, *Dogmatic Constitution on the Church [Lumen Gentium],* arts. 1, 4.

34   Matthew 7: 12.

35   Christoph Theobald, '"God is Relationship"; Some Recent Approaches to the Mystery of the Trinity', *God: Experience and Mystery,* edited by Werner Jeanrond and Christoph Theobald (*Concilium 2001/1*), pp. 45–57; p. 52.

36   Ibid.

37   Zamagni's essay on *Economics, Conscience and Globalisation* concludes as follows:

> The justice obtained through the use of force, even when it is legitimate, is never definitive, because there is no guarantee that the 'guilty' have repented ... Whereas forgiveness is at the same time the wiser and more rational act ... But to become capable of forgiveness we need to be able to give freely. So we need to put back into the centre of a strategy for institutional pacificism the culture of the gift, and hence of the gift economy

which is 'the most effective and most convincing vehicle' of 'that culture today' (p. 40).

38   I have failed to trace the source of that quotation, for which I apologize to the reader and to the late Archbishop. In an essay first published in 1989, reflecting on both the 1968 conference of Latin American bishops at Medellín and that held in 1979 at Puebla, Archbishop McGrath said of the final document produced by the latter:

> The fourth part speaks of *option*. Many options are scattered through the text of Puebla, but here, four

are highlighted, unevenly. The first, the preferential option for the poor, received attention, and it is found throughout the Puebla document: option for the poor themselves, and option for social and structural changes on their behalf. This option is, for some, necessarily and perhaps primarily political, even ideological; for others, it is highly and almost exclusively spiritual and eleemosynary, a position that Puebla rejects. Puebla's position springs from evangelization, and from this basis addresses the whole question of living a spirit of poverty in the church. It is this spirit of poverty that allows all members of the church to evangelize the poor and so to be evangelized by them; Puebla's position insists, on spiritual grounds, that drastic social and structural changes are required in the face of national and international injustices that create and widen the 'growing gap' between rich and poor that is, 'in the light of faith, a scandal and contradiction to our Christian condition'.

(Puebla, 28)

At the end of his essay, he remarks, of the situation at the time, a decade later, at which he writes:

> since Puebla, the problem of poverty – the 'widening gap' between rich and poor, 'a scandal and a contradiction for the Christian' (*Puebla*, 28) – has worsened and has been complicated by the oppressive foreign debt of many Latin American nations ... Our situation now is far more difficult than at the time of Puebla, and the gaps between rich and poor are far more severe.

See Archbishop Marcos McGrath, C.S.C., 'The Medellín and Puebla Conferences and their impact on the Latin American Church', in Edward Cleary (ed.), *Path from Puebla: Significant Documents of the Latin American Bishops since 1979* (Washington, D.C.: United States Catholic Conference, 1989), pp. 75–93, the cited passages being on pp. 90, 92; reissued as *Born of the Poor: The Latin American Church since Medellín* (Notre Dame: University of Notre Dame Press, 1990). I have quoted the Archbishop at some length because this volume seems unobtainable in Britain. I am most grateful to Judy Bartlet, of the Kellogg Institute, University of Notre Dame, and to Dominic Doyle, of Boston College, for tracking it down for me.

39   Herbert McCabe, *God Matters* (London: Geoffrey Chapman, 1987), p. 23.

40   Salley Vickers, *Miss Garnet's Angel*, p. 328.

Chapter 3

Cacophony and Conversation

Is Conversation Possible?

In Chapter 1, regretting the systemic failure of the Christian churches to understand themselves as schools of holiness, richly gifted projects of lifelong education, I said that we shall continue to misunderstand the kinds of 'project' that Judaism, Christianity and Islam purport to be unless we can recover the recognition that 'gods' are what you worship – whether or not you *name* as 'god' whatever it is on which, in fact, your heart is set – and that this most troublesome of words in our vocabulary is not, to put it paradoxically, the 'name' of God.

If, in accordance with the deepest and most consistent strands in Judaism, Christianity and Islam, we set ourselves to learn to worship, to learn to set our hearts upon, no fact or feature of the world; no institution, nation, individual; no value, theory, text or memory or dream, but only on the unknown and holy mystery from which all things come and to which all things are, through their healing, drawn; then we may be able better to appreciate how difficult it is to speak appropriately of God: for everything we say is metaphorically said. To try to speak of God is, unavoidably, to work with words and images carved from the world's wood, the territory of the familiar. All that we can do is, as Newman put it, to 'set right one error of expression by another', seeking thereby to 'steady our minds, not so as to reach their object, but to point them in the right direction'.[1]

In Chapter 2, I suggested that the intensifying phenomenon of 'globalization' – in economics, and politics, and communication – may at least bring the benefit of subverting the individualism which, in Western cultures (and especially in the most globally influential of them all: namely, the United States), so dangerously obscures from view the complex webs of relationship – relationships of production, of interaction, of influence and of responsibility – of which, in every word and thought and action, in all we are and say and do and suffer, we form a part. In the measure that modern individualism is subverted, we may learn, once again, the *primacy of relations* in the structure of the world.

Against this background, I devoted the rest of that chapter to indicating something of what would be implied by learning to understand all things as *given*, as expression of the giving that is God's identity, God's very self. I said something about holiness, about that gathering of humankind which we call 'Church', and about the appearance of God's life-givingness, God's Holy Spirit, as forgiveness, non-violence and the achievement of communion in the one world to which we all belong.

I have mentioned the need for what I called a 'global imagination', a sense of solidarity with the whole of humankind: past, present and future. It would, however, seem to be a necessary condition of the achievement and the fostering of such imagination that humankind could, in some measure, be brought into something like a common *conversation*.

That there are, in practice, immense – perhaps insuperable – difficulties standing in the way of such conversation is perfectly obvious. One has only to try to listen to the vast, conflictual diversity of voices emanating from Washington or Cairo; from Paris,

Beijing and New Delhi; from the heartlands of
Christian, or Muslim, or secular fundamentalism; from
the universities of Europe and the villages of Africa;
from the powerful and the dispossessed, the bankers
and the beggars and the bureaucrats. Listen to what
these voices variously say about the world, and about
what constitute the gravest dangers to its flourishing
and freedom: from this cacophony how could
conversation come?

In this chapter, I want to take that question as a way
in to some reflection on the second article of the Creed,
the article on Jesus Christ. Christianity has many ways
of referring the man who 'suffered under Pontius Pilate'
to the holy mystery of God, all of which (in orthodox
expression) proclaim that man's *identity* with God. As
the Nicene Creed puts it: he is 'God from God, light
from light, true God from true God'. Of all the
metaphors used to express this relationship, by far the
most familiar is, not 'light from light', but 'son from
father'. It is not, however, the language of parenthood
on which I shall concentrate, but rather that of
utterance: of the 'Word' that God is said to be, the Word
through whom 'all things came into being',[2] the Word
enfleshed from Bethlehem to Calvary. I shall do so under
four headings: first, the question that I have already
raised: 'Is Conversation Possible?'; then: 'Can We Put
Things into Words?'; third: 'Don't Speak Until You're
Spoken To' and, finally: 'Can Disaster Silence Speech?'

Many years ago, I found myself talking to an old
man who was working in a date plantation in the
northern Sahara, in Algeria (fortunately, we both spoke
reasonable French). He had, of course, never seen a
television set or entered a cinema. He had never been
north, across the Atlas Mountains; had never seen the
cities on the Mediterranean shore. 'Tell me', he said,
'what is the sea like?'

A first difficulty that stands in the way of global
conversation, even today, is the sheer diversity of our

experience as human beings: diversity of climate, of context, of labour, shaping the horizons of each person's world; diversity of the memories and stories and philosophies through which we variously interpret and, perhaps, reshape our world.

This first difficulty, the difficulty of understanding those whose experience, whose culture, may be profoundly different from one's own, is compounded by another: namely the extent to which different cultures, different contexts of conversation, exist not simply side by side, but are inextricably entangled in networks of economic and political relationship through which power is distributed with what is, far too often, quite literally devastating unevenness.

According to many people, however, the obstacles to global conversation go even deeper. Amartya Sen, the Nobel Prize-winning economist who was, until recently, Master of Trinity College, Cambridge, once referred to what he called the claim of 'cultural disharmony': the claim that 'people reared in different cultures may systematically lack basic sympathy and respect for each other. They may not even be able to understand one another, and could not possibly reason together.'[3] Notice that: could not *possibly*. In other words, there are influential thinkers (amongst whom, I hasten to add, Professor Sen is not himself to be numbered: he was merely reporting that such claims are made) according to whom global conversation is impossible not merely at present, in actual fact, but in principle. The philosophers call this suggestion the theory of 'incommensurable conceptual frameworks': the thesis that there are ways of seeing the world so different from each other that they lack any common basis from which comparison or interpretation might proceed. The American philosopher Donald Davidson saw this as a problem of the relationship between different *languages*, and he asked whether there might be 'languages which defy being translated into each other'.[4] Are some languages untranslatable – not just in respect of this or that feature of the world (as Fergus Kerr puts it: 'We may just have to learn Arabic if we want to understand camels. It is hard to do physics in Gaelic') – but from top to bottom? In other words, could there be 'a language which no stranger could ever learn'?[5]

Davidson's answer, which seems to me correct, is that there could not because if, as we watched those who made these sounds go about their business, we found ourselves *quite* unable to work out what was going on – quite unable to make well-formed guesses such as: 'Oh, *that* sound must mean "danger", *this* one "food"', and so on – then we should have no good reason to suppose that those who made these sounds were human beings.

So far, then, the suggestion is that conversation between human beings is possible, in principle, and hence that the notion of '*global* conversation' is, in principle, coherent, because the idea of radically incommensurable conceptual frameworks being inhabited by those who recognized each other to be human beings simply does not make sense.

All this talk of 'language', however, may mislead us into supposing that the recognition of our common humanity is something which first happens, as it were, 'inside our heads'; that 'recognition' is a mental act. There is, accordingly, a further step we need to take, and that is to acknowledge that it is our *bodiliness*, rather than our 'minds' (insofar as our minds are, misleadingly but frequently, considered something separate from our bodies), which grounds our ability, 'in principle, to learn any natural language on earth'.[6] When strange tribes meet, it is each other's physical behaviour that they observe, to which they react. The recognition that the stranger is a fellow human being entails an element of mutually acknowledged vulnerability, a requirement that a kind of *trust* be mutually offered – and accepted, or betrayed. (We might take the history of the handshake, the promise of the sword-free arm, as a parable of this.)

To sum up. Underlying the conviction that global conversation may be possible is an openness to the sharing of a common human *life* which is, in turn, grounded in an acknowledgement of mutual vulnerability, a common trust. Perhaps we could say that there are, anthropologically, few levels of meaning deeper, in the celebration of the Eucharist, than the celebration of life shared in the taking together of food and drink, although, of course, the heart of the matter, theologically, is that what is celebrated is the grounding of the possibility of such trust, such sharing, through the life-giving death and resurrection of the Crucified.

Ours is, at present, quite evidently a world in which such trust is, especially by the rich and powerful, regularly and systematically betrayed – from the countless millions that we spend each year on weapons of destruction to the nauseous spectacle (at first in the United States, but now, increasingly, in Britain as well) of wealthy middle-class communities being transformed into well-protected fortresses against the supposedly dangerous poor.

Can We Put Things into Words?

I now want to move the argument in a slightly different direction, by suggesting that, beneath the kinds of threat to common life and global conversation that I have just indicated, there may lie an even more fundamental betrayal of our humanity: what George Steiner has called the breaking of the contract or, perhaps we might say, 'covenant', between 'word and world'.[7]

Steiner's argument – in a book entitled *Real Presences: Is There Anything* in *What We Say?* – goes something like this. To be human is to be able to speak. But *serious* speech is speech in which the speaker acknowledges responsibility for uttering, for giving voice to, the world of which we are, as I would say, the 'speaking part'. In such speech, says Steiner, 'the relationship between word and world ... [is] held in trust. This is to say that it has been conceived and ... enacted as a relation of responsibility.' And he notes, in passing, in the first place, that 'to be responsible' is 'to answer *to* and to answer *for*' and, in the second, that even 'logic', which may seem a very cool and neutral notion, derives from '*Logos*', from the Word – the Word by which, according to Jews and Christians, all the world is made.[8]

If we are the speaking part of things, we are the speaking *part*: our ability to articulate, to voice, the sense and truth of things does not, as it were, 'disconnect' us from the world we voice. 'Language,' says Fergus Kerr, 'neither grew on human beings like hair nor did they sit down and invent it.'[9] The webs of cause and consequence, of interaction and relationship, which bind the world into a single, complex whole, become (in us) relationships of duty, of 'response-ability', the ability to say 'Yes' and 'No', to make our contribution to the story and the drama and the healing of the world.

Our ability to listen, and to speak, and hence our duty to do both things well, form part, we might say, of the 'shape', the form or nature, that we have, as human beings, over time acquired.

It is of course true that, as Steiner puts it, 'We are at liberty to say anything',[10] but whereas the frivolous nihilisms of postmodernity construe such liberty as licence (the tone is usually petulant: 'I can say what I *want!*') the liberty to say anything is better understood as the burden of our responsibility to attempt to speak the truth in an almost unbearably dark and complex, almost (it seems, at times) painfully illegible, and hence unutterable, world.

'I believe,' says Steiner, 'the matter of *music* to be central to that of the meanings of man.'[11] The world makes music before we do, and the music that we make is, as it were, an articulation of the music of the world, a giving *voice* to things. In the music that we make, the truth of things (if we make music well) sings, and celebrates, and weeps.

When was the contract broken? When did we first forget that we are *answerable* for everything we say; that our first duty is to *listen*, to be attentive to the truth of things, to the 'logic' or 'Logos-traces' of the world? Steiner's answer is that the contract between word and world 'is broken for the first time, in any thorough and consequent sense ... during the decades from the 1870s to the 1930s'.[12] Break the contract, betray the trust, abandon the burdensome and life-defining duty to seek to speak the truth, and the only options left to us seem to be those either of *silence* (which is where the so-called 'death of God' comes in) or of uncontrolled and playful chattering along the margins of the world. Playful, but by no means always cheerful: while much of the best of modern poetry and drama keeps quite close company with despair, this same despair is masked, not contradicted, by the garrulous self-indulgence of the rich.

Knowing very little, compared to Steiner, about modern literature, I am not in any good position to question his dating of the breaking of the contract. But surely the *seeds*, at least, were sown much further back, perhaps in medieval nominalism, undoubtedly in the emergence, in the seventeenth century, of characteristically modern, or 'Cartesian', forms of those disastrous dualisms – of mind and body, 'subjective' and 'objective', the 'inside' and the 'outside' of the world – with which our imagination and our speech are still diseased?

It is not the distinctions that we draw, between the many different kinds of speech there are, that do the damage. The drawing of such distinctions seems constitutive of civilization. What does the damage is, on the one hand, the collapsing of distinctions into quite unreal dichotomies between (for example) a 'science' which purports to speak about the world while saying nothing in the world about the speaker, and 'art' construed as pure expression, not of public truth, but of private feeling.

On the other hand, what such unreal splitting of the public and the private worlds quite overlooks is that we are *bodies*, and bodies live in space and time. And *time*. According to the American critic Frederic Jameson: 'One of the most significant symptoms of contemporary or postmodern North American society and culture ... [is] the loss of historicity.'[13]

'What happens to our sense of the human,' asks Archbishop Rowan Williams, 'when it is divorced from a grasp of the self as something realised *in time*?'[14] That question is asked in the Introduction of his little book, *Lost Icons: Reflections on Cultural Bereavement*, the argument of which points in a similar direction to that of Steiner's *Real Presences*.

Forgetfulness of temporality entails, in the last analysis, forgetfulness of God. According to Nietzsche, and many after him: 'Where God clings to our culture, to our routines of discourse, He is a fossil embedded in the childhood of rational speech ... This essay,' says Steiner, 'argues the reverse. It proposes that any coherent understanding of what language is, and how language performs ... is, in the last analysis, underwritten by the assumption of God's presence.'[15] And according to Rowan Williams, 'the issue finally raised', by his own essay, 'is whether a wholly secular language for the self can resist the trivialisations and reductions outlined in the book as a whole'.[16]

Steiner is highly critical of Wittgenstein, especially the Wittgenstein of the *Tractatus* – a text which ends, notoriously: 'Whereof one cannot speak, thereon one must remain silent.'[17] 'For the *Tractatus*,' says Steiner, 'the truly "human" being ... is he who keeps silent before the essential.'[18] Such insistence on 'keeping silent before the essential', now so pervasive in our society, may wear the masks of modesty or even 'mysticism' to disguise our abdication of responsibility. We 'keep silent' before God, and truth, and justice. We 'hold our peace' and, in this silence, millions starve and die.

We might, perhaps, put it like this. Speech that has forgotten that the fundamental form of speech is conversation; forgotten that to be able to converse with others is to have been schooled in a culture of relationships; forgotten that all conversation and all culture are, ultimately, answerable not only to each other but to God – such speech would, in the long run, cease to be speech at all and, with this cessation, its utterers would be less than human.

We might have supposed that, with the contract broken, with God forgotten, and silence kept about the things that really matter, we could settle for some modest, homespun humanism, some comfortable common sense. This is not, in fact, it seems, how things work out. Increasingly, in place of serious conversation, cacophony takes the form of an unholy and exceedingly dangerous combination of, on the one hand, strident and destructive *monologues* – the political, scientific and religious fundamentalisms that boom at us from every side – and, on the other, of what Steiner calls '*kitsch* ideologies'.[19]

No one ever said that serious speech was easy: merely that speech, response to the one Word through whose utterance all things are made, is what makes us the kinds of things we are, what makes us human beings, and hence that serious speech is our defining duty.

Things in time *take* time, and to take time is to be patient. The twin voices of contemporary evasion and despair: silence about things that matter, and chattering in the void, do not yet exhaust the possibilities. *Real Presences* ends with a moving sketch of what Steiner thinks of as the 'Saturday' condition of our time: the Saturday of the silence of the tomb; the Saturday between Good Friday, the time of waste, of interminable suffering, 'of the brute enigma of ending, which so largely make[s] up not only the historical dimension of the human condition, but the everyday fabric of our personal lives', and Easter Sunday, a time of 'comprehension, of resurrection, of a justice and a love that have conquered death'. But, says Steiner, 'ours is the long day's journey of the Saturday', a time of patience, in which appropriate speech – good music and good poetry, good conversation and responsible philosophy – will spring from 'an immensity of waiting'.[20] Not inactivity, but patience – which is the active form of hope.

'Don't Speak Until You're Spoken To'

As a small child (but, even then, loquacious!) I was always being told not to speak until I was spoken to. It was many years before I realized that, beneath the tedious discipline of the nursery, there lay a fundamental truth: nobody *can* speak until they're spoken to. As Saint Augustine put it: 'each one of us learnt our native language by habitually hearing it spoken.'[21] Each of us comes from somewhere: from some particular place, some tribe, some set of stories; we are the variously enriched and burdened, healed and wounded, product of some particular people; and we must help each other work out where we, and other people, are, and where to go, and how to get there. Truth is tradition-dependent, and learning how to speak the truth takes time.

And yet, this fundamental fact about the world is easy to forget. Amartya Sen, in the paper quoted earlier, takes issue with the fashionable 'communitarianism' in social thought, according to which 'one's identity is a matter of "discovery", not choice'. The view, he says, that 'a person's identity is something he or she detects rather than determines – would have been resisted' by no less an authority than the Emperor Akbar 'on the grounds that we do have a choice about our beliefs, associations and attitudes, and must take responsibility for what we actually choose'.[22]

I have visited the curious construction in Fatehpur Sikhri in which Akbar, seated on a central pillar, engaged in conversation with scholars and sages drawn from all the varied traditions that made up the Moghul Empire. I hope Professor Sen misreads him. I don't doubt for a moment that Akbar urged people to take responsibility for the choices that they made, but I hope that one of the wisest rulers of the sixteenth century did not fall into the trap of supposing discovery and decision, learning and making up one's own mind, to be *alternatives*: competing accounts of how we come to be the people that we are, of how we come to truth.

This is the dangerously unreal view which Western cultures have inherited from the Enlightenment; a view which Archbishop Rowan Williams has described as operating 'with a model of truth as something ultimately separable *in our minds* from the ... process of its historical reflection and appropriation'. Our impatience with debate, with difficulty, with ambivalence and paradox is, he says, 'at heart an impatience with learning, and with learning about our learning'.[23]

Learning to tell the truth takes time, attentiveness and patience. Good learning calls, no less than teaching does, for courtesy, respect, a kind of reverence: reverence for facts and people, evidence and argument, for climates of speech and patterns of behaviour different from our own. There are, I think, affinities (I put it no more strongly) between the courtesy, the attentiveness, required for friendship; the passionate disinterestedness without which no good scholarly or scientific work is done; and the contemplativity which strains, without credulity, to listen for the voice of God: who speaks the Word He is, but does not shout.[24]

To be human is to be able to speak, to say 'Yes' or 'No'; to be able to *respond* to places, times and people, and, perhaps, to God. George Steiner handles, with impressive honesty, the difficulty – in our supposedly 'post-religious' culture – of giving intelligible expression to the recognition that the possibility of speech is grounded in the possibility of prayer. Steiner puts it this way: 'the embarrassment we feel in bearing witness to the poetic, to the entrance into our lives of the mystery of otherness in art and in music, is of a metaphysical-religious kind.' If that seems to be making rather heavy weather of it, do not forget that the witness he is bearing is borne by one who would not, I think, easily classify himself as a believer. He goes on: 'What I need to state plainly here is both the prevailing convention of avoidance, and my personal incapacity, both intellectual and expressive, to overcome it adequately ... Yet the attempt at testimony must be made and the ridicule incurred. For what else are we talking about?'[25] In the present cultural climate, I find that quite courageous.

If, then, there is a sense in which the fundamental form of speech is prayer, response, *our* words' acknowledgement that all things come into being through the Word that is with God in the beginning, the Word that God is said to be, of what *kind* of prayer are we speaking? Of praise, for example, gratitude for all gifts given, or of petition, acknowledgement of need?

I remember, many years ago, having an animated debate about this with the Dominican theologian Herbert McCabe. I was arguing for praise, or gratitude, and Herbert for petition. Over the years, I have come to realize that the question was not well posed, the

alternatives unreal. What is at issue is the creature's
relation to the Creator, a relation which only human
beings, the speaking part of things, can *voice*. That
relation (as I intend to spell out in more detail in the
following chapter) is one of radical contingency, of
absolute dependence. Of ourselves we are, quite
literally, nothing. This might suggest that the
fundamental form of speech, of the 'voicing' or
articulation of this relationship, should indeed (as
McCabe argued) be that of petition, because we are in
need of absolutely everything. The creature is
absolutely beholden to the Creator.

And yet, there is something wrong here. We do not
need to *ask* for our existence. It is already given and,
for this gift, we should be grateful. It is as constituted
creatures with a context, an identity, a history, that we
express, articulate, give voice to, our creaturely
condition. If McCabe was not quite right, therefore, in
insisting that all prayer is grounded in petition, it does
not necessarily follow that I had the better argument,
and that it would be more accurate to say that the
fundamental form of prayer is gratitude for what we
have been given. Why not? Because the language of
gratitude and praise does not, in itself, sufficiently
express the enduring absoluteness of contingency, the
permanence of our complete dependence upon the
mystery of God. Moreover, neither answer, neither
'praise' nor 'petition', makes mention of the connection
between our relationship to God and our relations with
each other, and yet the latter are, of course, the
expression of the former (as the twenty-fifth chapter of
Saint Matthew's Gospel spells out at some length).

The fundamental form of speech is prayer. What
kind of prayer? I suggest that we might call it
'contemplation', as defined by Rowan Williams:
'Contemplation', he says, 'is a deeper appropriation of
the vulnerability of the self in the midst of the language
and transactions of the world.'[26] The notion of

'vulnerability' neatly combines recognition of contingency, of the creature's absolute dependence on the mystery of God, with a point that I made earlier in this chapter, to the effect that the possibility of global conversation is grounded in openness to the sharing of common human life which is, in turn, grounded in acknowledgement of mutual vulnerability, of common trust. To be human is to be able to speak. But to be able to speak is to be 'answerable', 'response-able' to and for each other, and to the mystery of God. But are there circumstances in which speech becomes impossible? This is the last question that I want to consider in this chapter: can disaster silence speech?

Can Disaster Silence Speech?

Silence may take many forms. There is the silence of those who have nothing to say; there is the silence of despair; there is the silence in which human beings are held in love and wonder. There is also, as we have seen, the silence of those who, lacking the courage to act or speak, 'hold their peace' while others starve and die.

It is not with any of these kinds of silence that I am concerned. Is there, at the darkest edge of things, a silence that is not something which we choose to do, but rather something done to us? (This is, perhaps, one way of reading Hamlet's final words: 'The rest is silence.') All dying silences, of course, but we are animals and, as such, have only so much time in which to live and speak. Mortality does not, of itself, unravel meaning, subvert speech. Death is not, in itself, disastrous – and it is with speech quite silenced by disaster that I am concerned.

It has become a cliché to suggest that the Holocaust made it impossible to speak of God. The Holocaust certainly made glibness, the cloaking with platitude of what Conrad called the 'heart of darkness', quite

obscene. For this we should be grateful. If we open our
mind's eye, make vulnerable our imagination, to the
sheer *scale* of the suffering inflicted by human beings on
each other – from Auschwitz to Rwanda, from
Passchendaele to AIDS in Africa and to the
consequences, largely unnoticed by the rich and
powerful, of the havoc wreaked upon the poor by the
way we work the markets of the world – then *easy*
speech concerning peace, and love, and harmony (and
God) is silenced from the start.[27]

'My subject is War, and the pity of War,' said Wilfred
Owen, in the Preface to his *Collected Poems*. He went
on: 'All a poet can do today is warn. That is why the
true poets must be truthful.'[28] Owen's own Christian
faith did not survive the suffering that he saw. He
refused, however, to be silenced. If, in such
circumstances, it remains the duty of the poet to be
truthful, to issue warnings, then surely every Jew and
every Christian finds themselves called to exercise, in
some measure, the duty of the poet?

This chapter, I said at the beginning, would reflect
upon the second article of the Creed, in which
Christians confess their faith in God as Jesus Christ, the
crucified and risen One. I may seem hardly to have
done what I set out to do! I did, however, also say that
I would focus on the metaphor, not of 'sonship', but of
'utterance', considering the 'Word' that God is said to
be.

God does not say many things, but one. God speaks
the one Word that God is and, in that one Word's
utterance, all things come into being, find life and shape
and history and, in due time, find fullest focus, form
and flesh, in Mary's child. The Prologue to the Fourth
Gospel is not, by any means, all about Jesus, but it *is*,
from start to finish, about the one Word that God is,
about the utterance through which all things came into
being: the utterance which, if heard as it is here
proclaimed, invites the confession that Jesus is the

Christ, the man from Nazareth is God's one Word made flesh.

God does not say many things, but one. That is not an arithmetical statement, but a reading rule: it tells you how to read the Scriptures. It can hardly be an arithmetical statement because, in the first chapter of Genesis alone (the chapter which the Johannine Prologue, as it were, 'reissues') God says all manner of things: 'God said' this, and 'God said' that; 'God called the dry land Earth, and the waters that were gathered together he called Seas'; 'God blessed them, and God said to them: "Be fruitful and multiply"', and so on.[29] And goodness knows how many times, in Scripture, the prophets bear witness to the different things 'God says'.

And yet, God says not many things, but one, uttering the one Word that God is. That is how, as Christians, we are to read the Scriptures, and that is the story told in the Fourth Gospel's Prologue: 'In the beginning was the Word ... and we have seen his glory, the glory as of a father's only son, full of grace and truth.'[30]

If I have concentrated, so far in this chapter, on what we might call 'utterance in general', and on the relationship between our utterances and the utterance that is God, the Word, I have done so in part as a corrective to our tendency to consider christological questions in isolation from their context in the whole sweep of history, culture and creation.

Nevertheless, if we are going to treat the question 'Can disaster silence speech?' with the seriousness which it deserves, we need to focus it more sharply than I have done so far. We need to ask: Can disaster silence *God's* speech, can it reduce *God's* Word to silence? The question may seem, at worst, blasphemous or, at best, quite foolish. Before dismissing it, however, let us briefly consider the passion narrative in Mark's Gospel.

Does God suffer? To suffer is to undergo some change. There are those who say that, if God does *not* suffer, then He must be most unfeeling, quite lacking in compassion. But, God does not change, not because he is unfeeling but because he is, eternally, pure generosity, absolute donation, endlessly creative love. True love does not change, is not capricious, and God is love. God does not suffer and yet, we say God died on Calvary.

I am not playing academic word games, but reminding us how important, and how difficult, it is to be clear about the appropriate registers of language that we use in our attempts to speak of God. In the New Testament, 'ὁ θεος' ('God' with the definite article) refers, almost invariably, to the Father,[31] whereas, when *we* say 'God', we may – depending on the context – be speaking of the Father, or the Spirit, or the Son, or, simultaneously, of Father, Son and Spirit. The Father did not die on Calvary, but the Son did, in the death of Jesus. Or, to change the metaphor: eternally, unquenchably, God utters, but must we not say that, in the death of Jesus, God's utterance was silenced?

The Gospels are not biographies of Jesus but announcements of who he is and what, in him, God is doing. There is hardly a line in the Gospels which does not need to be read alongside whichever passage in the *Old* Testament the evangelist is declaring, at this point, to be fulfilled.

'My God, my God, why have you forsaken me?': the great cry from the Cross is from Psalm 21. Then, two verses later: 'someone ran, filled a sponge with [vinegar], put it on a stick, and gave it to him to drink.' Now the allusion is to Psalm 69: 'Insults have broken my heart, so that I am in despair. I looked for pity, but there was none; and for comforters, but I found none. They gave me poison for food, and for my thirst they gave me vinegar to drink.'[32]

But, if we go back a few verses in that Psalm, we read:

But as for me, my prayer is to you, O Lord. At an acceptable time, O God, in the abundance of your steadfast love, answer me. With your faithful help rescue me from sinking in the mire; let me be delivered from my enemies and from the deep waters. Do not let the flood sweep over me, or the deep swallow me up.[33]

We are back at the first chapter of Genesis; back at the creation of the world; back at the watery chaos from which, by God's utterance, the world was made and to which, in Noah's day, the sin of humankind nearly consigned it once again.

In other words, what Mark is doing, with his use of this Old Testament material, is to suggest that, in Jesus' dying, the Word that makes and orders all the things there are is *itself* threatened by the chaos-waters which were, 'in the beginning', by that Word set in their place. At this point, the Gospel becomes almost intolerably paradoxical because, to hear this text *as* 'gospel', as declaration of 'good news', is to confess, in fear and trembling, that the pain and darkness of the world go right down to the very heart of things, silencing God's own speech, and yet, that in that dreadful silence, the world is made again: there is a 'new creation'.

By way of conclusion, therefore, something must be said about how, after Calvary (or 'after Auschwitz', or after each and every eruption of the darkness with which wickedness corrupts the world, for all this darkness is, for the Christian, to be read through Calvary's lens), we may, nevertheless, learn to speak again.

Learning to Speak Again

The darkness of the world is beyond all explanation – which is why we speak about the 'mystery' of evil. We too often forget, however, that *goodness* is a mystery as well; that kindness, generosity, the 'giftness' of reality,

is (as I argued in the previous chapter) beyond all
explanation. 'Religious thought and practice', says
George Steiner, 'make narrative images of the
rendezvous of the human psyche with absolute
otherness, with the strangeness of evil or the deeper
strangeness of grace.'[34]

I like that: the deeper strangeness of grace. The one
example of such a 'rendezvous' which Steiner mentions
in that passage is the meeting on the road to Emmaus.
There is, I believe, an immensely important lesson to be
learned from the emphasis which all the gospels place
upon the difficulty which the disciples experienced in
recognizing the risen Christ. What does God look like?
The figure hanging on the crucifix. But to recognize this
figure as the human face of *God* is thereby to recognize
the risen Christ.

The disciples on the road to Emmaus were not,
strictly speaking, silenced by the shattering disaster of
Jesus' crucifixion. As they walked those 'seven miles',
they were 'talking with each other about all these things
that had happened'.[35]

But they don't know what to say. The stranger who
joins them on the road does not change the facts. 'Jesus
of Nazareth who was a prophet mighty in deed and
word before God and all the people' (as they tell the
stranger – a typical piece of Christian behaviour: telling
God who he is!); Jesus of Nazareth remains, as they say,
'condemned to death and crucified'.[36]

What the stranger does, as he takes them back
through the history of Israel, and the Scriptures which
they thought they knew so well, is to give them an
entirely new sense of what has been going on. 'Were not
our hearts burning within us?'[37] they say later, as they
gradually began to see the point; began, we might say,
to speak a quite new language, to glimpse a world quite
different from the world they thought they knew.

At the end of the road, the context is one of
hospitality: they invite the stranger in. He is the guest;

they are his hosts. At least, this would have been so, in the old language, in the world which died on Calvary. What they discover, when they are at table, is that it is *they*, in fact, who are the guests, recipients of hospitality; and that it is *he* who is the host.

And then, at last, 'they recognized him; and he vanished from their sight'.[38] That last phrase is, perhaps, misleading, because the one who 'vanished' was the kind of man you meet along the road: one in the figure of a human being bounded, as all human beings are, by mortality. What they 'recognized', as they began to see the point, was his new presence as the bread he broke, the life he shared, at the beginning of this new conversation which is, for all eternity, uninterruptible.

Notes

1   Newman, *Theological Papers on Faith and Certainty*, p. 102.
2   John 1: 3.
3   Amartya Sen, 'East and West: the reach of reason', *The Moral Universe*, pp. 19–33; p. 25.
4   Donald Davidson, 'On the very idea of a conceptual scheme'; Chapter 13 of Davidson, *Inquiries into Truth and Interpretation* (Oxford: Clarendon Press, 1984), paraphrased and glossed by Fergus Kerr, *Theology after Wittgenstein* (Oxford: Basil Blackwell, 1986), p. 106.
5   Kerr, op. cit., p. 106.
6   Ibid., p. 109, paraphrasing Wittgenstein.
7   George Steiner, *Real Presences: Is There Anything* in *What We Say?* (London: Faber and Faber, 1989), p. 89.
8   Ibid., p. 90 (my stress); cf. p. 89.
9   Kerr, *Theology after Wittgenstein*, p. 114.
10   Steiner, *Real Presences*, p. 53.
11   Ibid., p. 6 (my stress).
12   Ibid., p. 93.
13   Frederic R. Jameson, 'On *Habits of the Heart*', *Community in America*, edited and introduced by Charles H. Reynolds and Ralph U. Norman (Berkeley: University of California Press, 1988), p. 104.

14 Rowan Williams, _Lost Icons: Reflections on Cultural Bereavement_ (Edinburgh: T. & T. Clark, 2000), p. 5.
15 Steiner, _Real Presences_, p. 3.
16 Williams, _Lost Icons_, p. 7.
17 Ludwig Wittgenstein, _Tractatus Logico-Philosophicus_, translated by D. F. Pears and B. F. McGuiness (London: Routledge and Kegan Paul, 1961), p. 7.
18 Steiner, _Real Presences_, p. 103.
19 Ibid., p. 230.
20 Ibid., p. 232. For some more extended reflection on Steiner's suggestive little book, the reader might turn to the Aquinas Lecture which I delivered in Blackfriars, Cambridge, in January 1990: 'Friday, Saturday, Sunday', _New Blackfriars_ (March 1990), pp. 109–119. I ended that lecture as follows:

> My colleague Stephen Sykes recently set his seminar to spend a term discussing a book of mine called _Easter in Ordinary_. As they talked about it, one member of the seminar (I am told) suggested that any future edition should be retitled 'Easter on Saturday'. I think that is rather a good idea! But best of all, perhaps, would be to call it 'Easter Vigil', in order to indicate the sense in which all prayer and expectation, all keeping of createdness in mind, occur on Saturday, in darkness illuminated from the pain of God, in watchfulness for the rising of the sun, in patience.
>
> (pp. 118–119).

21 Augustine, _On Christian Teaching_, translated by R. P. H. Green (Oxford: Oxford University Press, 1997), p. 8.
22 Sen, 'East and West', p. 32.
23 Rowan Williams, _On Christian Theology_ (Oxford: Blackwell, 2000), p. 132.
24 See Lash, _Believing Three Ways in One God_, pp. 10–11.
25 Steiner, _Real Presences_, p. 178.
26 Rowan Williams, 'Theological Integrity', _New Blackfriars_ 72 (1991), p. 148, my stress.
27 Remember G. K. Chesterton's prayer that the 'good Lord' should 'deliver us' from 'the easy speeches that comfort cruel men'.
28 Owen, _The Collected Poems of Wilfred Owen_, edited by C. Day Lewis (London: Chatto & Windus, 1963), p. 31.
29 In that first account of the creation (Genesis 1–2: 3) 'God said' occurs ten times, 'God called' five times, and

'God blessed' thrice (once in the form 'God blessed them, saying').

30   John 1: 1, 14.

31   See Karl Rahner, 'Theos in the New Testament', *Theological Investigations,* Volume I, translated with an Introduction by Cornelius Ernst (London and Baltimore: Darton, Longman and Todd, and Helicon Press, 1961), pp. 79–148.

32   Mark 15: 34 (Psalm 21: 2); Mark 15: 36 (the New Revised Standard Version, pedantically, has 'sour wine', which loses the allusion); Psalm 69: 20–21.

33   Psalm 69: 13–15.

34   Steiner, *Real Presences,* p. 147.

35   Luke 24: 13, 14.

36   Luke 24: 19, 20.

37   Luke 24: 32.

38   Luke 24: 31.

Chapter 4

Attending to Silence

'Silence Belongs to the Father'

Towards the end of the last chapter, I referred to that very heart of darkness which is the silencing of God's Word, on Calvary. The paradoxes are intense, and to speak of them appropriately would require a poet's gifts, which I do not possess. We cannot speak unless we are spoken to; all speech is, in the last resort, response, and we are responsible for what we say. Yet what we *hear*, as we attempt to speak, is silence.

The paradigm is the garden of Gethsemane. 'Abba, Father, for you all things are possible; remove this cup from me; yet not what I want, but what you want.'[1] (The reader should forget those sentimental sermons in which Jesus' use of the Aramaic diminutive 'Abba', rendered by the preacher as 'Daddy', is offered in evidence of the intimacy of relationship between Son and Father, as if that intimacy could be construed as a kind of cosiness. In the starkest possible contrast to the impression thus created, this passage in Mark, depicting the agonizing and unanswering darkness of the garden, is, in fact, the only place in the gospels in which the term occurs.) Jesus speaks and, when he has spoken, there is silence. There is no suggestion, in the structure of the narrative, that he expected a reply. We are in completely different territory – from both a literary and a theological point of view – from the Book of Job in which, eventually, and devastatingly: 'the Lord answered Job out of the whirlwind'.[2] In Gethsemane there is no divine fulmination, no thunderous theophany. Jewish and Christian understanding of God has now reached the point where we do not expect, nor do we have any reason to suppose that Jesus expected, a reply. His duty, his obedience, goes all the way into the dark; his whole identity is given over into silence.

It is, after all, *Jesus* who is confessed to be God's Word made flesh; it is his life, and history, and destiny, that speak to us, inviting our response. There is no other word in God but this one Word which finds fully focused form and expression, in the created order, in the history of the Crucified. Nothing, therefore, is to be gained by attempting, as it were, to listen to something else, to listen 'beyond' Jesus, for some *other* word than that which he is said to be. What, we might say, would God utter, but his *Word*? We hear that Word in Jesus' agonizing cry into the darkness. As the German theologian Christoph Theobald puts it: 'silence belongs to the Father.'[3]

That expression may serve as the motto for this final chapter, as a reminder that, the closer we are drawn to God, the more that we begin to gain some understanding of the holy mystery of God, the more that what we are and what we say and what we do refracts the character of God's Word, the more conscious we become of the depths of our unknowing. God becomes *more* unknown, not less, the more we understand Him. This is why the tradition speaks of '*docta ignorantia*'; of 'educated ignorance'.[4]

The third article of the Creed (on which Chapter 2 was focused) confesses Christian faith in God as mystery of lifegiving holiness, as 'Holy Spirit'; the second (which we considered in Chapter 3) on God as utterance, as 'Word'. Finally, therefore, we turn to the first article of the Creed, confessing God as mystery of all things' origination, as 'Creator'. What is at issue in confessing ourselves, and everything there is in all the worlds there are, to be not merely facts but *creatures*, is, I shall suggest, a matter of learning to attend to silence.

Why was Pascal Afraid?

Some years ago, I took part in a conference, hosted by the Vatican Observatory, of physicists, philosophers and theologians. A Jesuit astronomer asked me: 'What is it that you learn, as a theologian, from the natural sciences?' I found it a surprisingly difficult question to answer. At one level, of course, the answer might have been: 'What any non-specialist learns of some subject from its specialists!' But that might have seemed evasive so, with his own discipline in mind, I replied: 'The sheer, unimaginable *vastness* of the world.' And I meant just that: unimaginable. I can learn from the astronomer that there are 4.4 light years between the sun and its nearest neighbour in our galaxy (which comes to 41.6 x 10^{12} kilometres), or that 50 million light years (roughly 208 x 10^{13} kilometres) separates our galaxy from galaxy M87 in the Virgo cluster, and so on. But, for the non-cosmologist like myself, great strings of zeros soon cease to be informative. Bearing them in mind, one does better, I suspect, by going out 'into the wilderness', leaving (so far as possible!) the city lights behind, on a clear night, with a good pair of binoculars.

Blaise Pascal was born in 1623, nineteen years before Isaac Newton. It was, therefore, in a Europe becoming rapidly aware, to an unprecedented degree, of the vastness of the universe, that Pascal wrote: 'le silence éternel de ces espaces infinies m'effraie': 'the eternal silence of these infinite spaces *terrifies* me'.[5]

Notice, however, that it was not the sheer size of 'these infinite spaces' which so unnerved the great mathematician, but their *silence*. The empty stillness of the sky speaks silently to human solitude. It is, I think, this sense of solitude that is unnerving. I have a suspicion (since the mathematics, on their own, point neither one way nor another) that one reason why some scientists seem so keen to suppose that *somewhere*, in some vastly distant region, there must be that which we could recognize as 'living', and as capable of communicating with us, is that – were these strange things friend or foe – meeting them would give us company, diminish our terrifying isolation. Other people, of course, will populate the distant skies with spirits, comfortable deities who may watch over us and protect us from the void.

If, however, we eschew all such purely speculative strategies of evasion, then we are left where Pascal stood: trembling before the terrifying silence of the world. The question that I want to ask, however, is this: is Pascal's terror *reasonable*?

On a narrow, purely calculative account of the criteria for rational behaviour, the answer, I suppose, is: No. He should have had a stiff drink, told himself to calm down and get on with measuring the distances. What there is is what there is, and that's an end to it.

If one knows anything of the working habits of great scientists, however, that seems less than satisfactory. Mathematicians, notoriously, have a highly developed sense of the aesthetic: the *beauty* of a good equation matters a great deal to them. And the cosmologists I know approach their work with (in my experience) not fear, indeed, but certainly with wonder: with a kind of reverence.[6]

I am not smuggling in an illegitimate exercise in what is now called 'natural theology' (a phrase first coined, incidentally, in 1670). I am only suggesting that, even if the scientist has no way, as a scientist, of answering the question (because it is not a scientific question), he or she is not abandoning the rationality proper to their enterprise in asking, with a kind of wonder: 'How come? What is all this *about*?' It does not surprise me, in other words, that, from the time of the Psalmist to the seventeenth century and even our own day, reflecting in wonder on the world has led human beings to formulate the kind of question which, in Jewish and in Christian discourse, is called the question of creation.

An End of Explanation

The world is what there is: from the most distant galaxy to the most minute convolutions of the human brain; from quarks and fractals to today's exchange rate; from the American and British invasion of Iraq in 2003 to Beethoven's late string quartets. The world is all the things there are.

What everybody calls 'the world', Jews and Christians also call 'creation', which confuses things, because cosmologists also speak sometimes of 'creation' but, when they do, they are not referring to the world, but to the establishment of its initial conditions.

Here, for example, is the late Professor Carl Sagan, concluding his Introduction to Stephen Hawking's *Brief History of Time*:

> This is also a book about God ... or perhaps about the absence of God. The word God fills these pages ... And this makes all the more unexpected the conclusion of the effort, at least so far: a universe with no edge in space, no beginning or end in time, *and nothing for a Creator to do.*[7]

Sagan, in other words, took it for granted that the concept of 'creation' functions, in Jewish and Christian thought, as an explanation of the establishment of the initial conditions of the world.

There are two issues here: the first concerns the notion of 'beginning', and the second concerns the sense in which creation might or might not be said to be 'something for God to do': the sense in which God can or cannot be said to be, straightforwardly, the 'maker of the world'. (The first line of the ancient Office hymn, '*Conditor alme siderum*', which I suppose might be rendered, very literally, as: 'kindly establisher of stars' [or 'skies'], runs, in one well-known nineteenth-century translation: 'Dear *maker* of the starry skies'.) Let me now say a word about each of these issues in turn.

The book of 'beginnings', the Book of Genesis, begins like this: 'In the beginning when God created the heavens and the earth, the earth was a formless void and darkness covered the face of the deep, while a wind from God swept over the face of the waters.'[8]

This is, as it were, 'Scene I'. It is a scene of dark and shapeless chaos, which God begins to order: 'Then God said, "Let there be light".' The story is not about the establishment of the initial conditions of the world (it does not, for example, ask: 'How did the darkness and the formless void come about; how did *they* "begin"?'); its focus is on the twofold claim – in rebuttal of the cosmic dualisms prevailing in neighbouring cultures – that the God of Israel is in charge of everything, is absolutely in control of everything there is, and that everything God does is good.

It was, I think, the American Old Testament scholar Bruce Vawter who said: 'to the Hebrew mind, what is true in principle, is true in the beginning'. In other words, the temporal image of 'beginning', in the Book of Genesis and elsewhere in the Hebrew Scriptures, expresses a truth more fundamental than mere matters of sequence or chronology: namely, the absolute dependence of everything on God. In the centuries that followed, a later Judaism and early Christianity sharpened or focused this conviction into the assertion that God creates all things out of *nothing*: '*ex nihilo*'.

Notice that I say: 'creates', in the present tense, and not 'created'. In contrast to the 'clockmaker' deisms of the Enlightenment, in which God simply sets things going, mainstream Christian theologies of creation – from Augustine and Aquinas to Karl Rahner or Karl Barth – have little interest in the temporal connotations of 'beginning'. Everything that God does that is not God, everything that God creates – galaxies and gases, promises and symphonies, bird-life and Milton Keynes – is, from its first instant to its last, out of *nothing* made.

In other words, the Jewish and Christian doctrine of creation has a *history*: it developed from an ancient Near-Eastern cosmogony resistant to the prevailing dualisms of struggling light and dark, of good and evil locked in endless conflict, into the recognition that absolutely everything is radically contingent, need not have been at all, and that its being is a kind of gift, an act of kindness, an emergent mystery of peace and harmony. (Notice, however, that, on this account, developed doctrines of creation are about the future quite as much as they are about the past, for 'peace and harmony' are not the way that most things are today or ever yet have been: they are the way that God's creating gift of everything will one day be, in its achievement.)

But the account of creation offered by modern science has *also* had a history. In the seventeenth century, it seemed as if the system of the world required some single, overarching principle of explanation – some ultimate and fundamental *cause*. It is not at all surprising that this quest was assumed, by those who undertook it, to be a secular or scientific version of the doctrine of creation: after all, what could the 'world-cause' *be*, but God?

As time went on, it was gradually understood that the world did not require any such single, ultimate, explanatory principle, and scientists, losing interest in the concept of a '*causa mundi*', thereby lost interest in God (as Laplace put it: 'We have no need of that hypothesis'[9]). According to the Scottish Astronomer

Royal, writing in 1983: 'When we speak of the "beginning" of the Universe, we always mean the time to which we can trace back ultimately all the various phenomena which we now observe.' And he went on to quote Sir Edmund Whittaker, who had said, in 1942, that, when we do so, then, 'by purely scientific methods ... we arrive ultimately at a critical state of affairs beyond which the laws of nature, as we know them, cannot have operated: a Creation, in fact'.[10]

Notice that '*beyond* which'. Whittaker's universe has an 'edge', 'beyond which' something may be going on. And it is this sense, of the 'beginning' of the world as a kind of edge or *boundary*, itself requiring explanation, which Carl Sagan, in the passage that I quoted earlier, suggests that recent developments in cosmology have set aside. Hence his reference to 'a universe with no *edge* in space' and 'no *beginning* in time'. That way of putting it, however, simply perpetuates confusion. If space and time are 'bounded', then the 'edge of space' would not be an 'edge *in* space'; a 'beginning of time' would not be a 'beginning *in* time'. The point is not unimportant: as Saint Augustine saw, way back in the fourth century, it stops us asking questions such as, 'What was God doing *before* he made the world?', to which he is said to have replied: 'He was creating hell for people who ask silly questions like that!'

So much for the notion of 'beginning'. Next: what about the sense in which God did or did not 'make' the world? Making is a kind of causing, a way of bringing things about: we make windowpanes and war; we make mushroom soup and sometimes make amends. All these are processes, the achieving in time of outcomes and effects. Explanations are stories of causes and effects and, as I mentioned in Chapter 1, explanations, if successful, have an end.

There is, however, no story, and hence no explanation, that *begins* with 'nothing'. Try it some time: try telling a story that begins with your mind completely blank. From nothing, from nothing *whatsoever*, you cannot ask the question: 'And then, what happened *next*?' If, then, God creates the world *ex nihilo*, out of nothing, God is not the *explanation* of the world. And, if God is not the explanation of the world, then creating (out of nothing) is not a kind of making.

Whereas the Genesis story has God shaping chaos, in the developed Jewish and Christian doctrines of creation, creating is not, in fact, a 'shaping', because there is nothing there to shape. 'Creation', as Rowan Williams puts it, 'is *no sort of process*' because it is not a kind of *change*. Changes are only brought about in things and situations which were there before the change began. 'The existence of the world', Williams goes on, 'is not a puzzling fact, as opposed to other, straightforward facts'; the existence of the world is 'all the facts there are'.[11] And to confess the world to be created is to confess that all the facts there are depend upon the mystery that we call God.

If God is not the explanation of the world, and if creating out of nothing is not a kind of making because it does not entail a change of any kind, then why does the tradition speak of God as 'cause' at all?

When we speak, these days, of 'causing' things, we *only* think of making them, of bringing them about. In contrast, medieval scholars used the language of causation in a much more varied, we might say metaphorically related, range of ways. Thus, for example, the *purpose* of an object or an act would count amongst its 'causes'. 'What's that for?' you might ask, pointing to a curious attachment to a Swiss Army knife. 'It's for taking stones out of horses' hooves.' That's what it's for; that is its purpose, what would once have been called its 'final cause'.

How did this happen? What's this for? What is this shaped like? What is it made of? In medieval thought, all such enquiries would have counted as searching for causes. And when the concept of causation was used in so many very different, if related, ways, it was not all that difficult to stretch its use still further, and find a place for it in our attempts to speak of the relationship of all things to almighty God.

That is the first point, but the second would be that, *when* they did so, medieval thinkers knew full well that they were putting the notion to new use. They watched their language with great care as they extended the metaphorical range of the concept of causation to say that, in some sense, 'creating' is a kind of 'causing'. (When Aquinas, in the First Part of the *Summa*, having completed his discussion of the mystery of God, turns to the consideration of God's relationship to creatures, the very first question that he tackles concerns the various different senses in which God may be said to be the 'cause' of everything there is.[12])

If we are creatures, then we are created. But how are we to speak about the mystery of our creation? As I was at pains to emphasize in Chapter 1, everything that human beings say of the Creator is said in words and images carved from the fabric of the world that the Creator makes. Everything that is said of God, whether in affirmation or denial, is anthropomorphically expressed. To speak appropriately of the holy mystery that makes and heals the world, but is not the world nor any item in it, is quite beyond the resources of language. It is the tragedy of modern Western culture to have fallen victim to the illusion (widely shared by believer and nonbeliever alike) that it is perfectly easy to talk about God.

As I mentioned in that first chapter, each of the great religious traditions of the world has its own procedures for protecting us from the illusion that the Holy One can be pinned down, classified, given any proper name. 'Not this, not that': the disciplining of imagination, far from being the exclusive prerogative of Buddhism, or of some esoteric group of specialists called 'mystics', is and always has been at the heart of serious speech and appropriate behaviour in Hinduism as in Judaism, in Islam as in Christianity.

Concerning creation's relationship to the Creator, Christians, we might say, know four things.

They know that they, and all things, are *created*.

They know that they, and all things, are *lovingly* created.

They know that they, and all things, are lovingly created into *peace*.

Finally, they know that that is *all* they know. The rest is the attempt to gain some understanding of the things we know.

But how do we learn all this?

Contingency as Gift

'God', said Hegel, 'does not offer himself for observation.'[13] He was not saying that knowledge of God is impossible, but that it is not the *kind* of knowledge at which scientists and historians aim, as they put some feature of the world, or some episode from human history, under the microscope of academic scrutiny. The objects of such scrutiny are, shall we say, inert, picked up with tweezers, inspected, classified, conceptually controlled. God is not such an object.

It follows that, if some knowledge of God is attainable by human beings, the *route* towards it will not be the path of academic – scientific or philosophical – enquiry (this is not to deny that knowledge gained in ways other than the academic should be critically tested, checked, examined – as all knowledge-claims may be – but that is a different matter).

Perhaps a quick comment on the concept of 'natural theology' may be helpful here. The notion of 'natural theology' makes its first appearance (as I mentioned earlier) in 1670, and this characteristically early modern project conflates two quite different enterprises. On the one hand, there is the 'grammatical', or philosophical, activity of reflecting on, and puzzling over, our uses of the word 'god'. This honourable enterprise, whose roots lie buried in antiquity, is the kind of thing Aquinas was referring to when he spoke of 'that theology [or "god-talk"] which is part of philosophy'.[14] On the other hand, there was the much more dubious business of attempting to demonstrate, whether *a priori* or by empirical investigation, that, over and above the world, there is, 'beyond' the world, a further object known as 'God'. It is the latter enterprise that is the target of Hegel's remark.

There is, in certain scientific circles, a reductionism abroad according to which the *only* road to knowledge is that mapped out by techniques of enquiry which are today deemed 'scientific'. But this, of course, is nonsense. Most of the things that most people know, they have not learned this way. There is an irreducible diversity of ways in which, as human beings, we feel our way towards the truth.

Where the knowledge of God is concerned, most (though not all) of the major religious traditions of the world have sought in *personal* knowledge – in the knowledge that human beings acquire of themselves and of each other through networks of relationship – the least inappropriate analogy or metaphor that we have for the character of the relations between human beings and God (hence the centrality, in what we say of God, of motifs such as 'gift' and 'utterance', on which we concentrated in the two previous chapters). And thus it is that Judaism, Christianity and Islam, while insisting on the absoluteness of the difference between the creature and the Creator, and hence on the radical incomprehensibility of the mystery of God, whose unknownness deepens in proportion that we know Him better, characteristically speak of God in personal terms.

The world does not tell us that it is created. But the world does leave us with a question. It is, as I said earlier, not a scientific question, not a question about some feature of the world, about its distance, size or character. It is simply the question: how come *anything*? What is this all *about*? It is a question which we seek to formulate when we are moved to wonder by the sheer fact of the world's existence.

It must be admitted that, from a logical point of view, the question: 'How come that there is something, rather than nothing?' is very curious. (How does the comparative 'rather than' work, except by smuggling in a notion of 'nothing' as a kind of thing?) It is not, I think, surprising that many serious and distinguished thinkers (including, notoriously, Bertrand Russell) have insisted that the question is, in fact, quite unintelligible. And, of course, if it is unintelligible, if we have absolutely no idea as to what could count as an answer to it, then it is not a question to which there is no answer; it simply is not (in spite of its grammatical appearance) a *question* at all: it's just gibberish. Thus it is that Russell, and those who think like him, rest content with the assertion that the world is simply *there* and that's an end to it.

However, that everything there is is just brute fact is not, itself, a further fact about the world (that was the point of Rowan Williams' insistence that the existence of the world is not a further, 'puzzling' fact about the world, over and above all the familiar facts there are). To say that everything there is is just brute fact is one way of telling a most sophisticated story: a story which, while by no means self-evidently false, is not self-evidently true. We learn such stories, and discern their truth and adequacy, by being participants in cultural contexts which entertain them and, perhaps, endorse them, embodying them in social practices.

The same is true, of course, about the route which
Russell rejected. To take the question: 'How come there
is anything rather than nothing?' *seriously*, seriously to
explore its intelligibility; to acknowledge the issue of
radical contingency to be extremely interesting; to take
it as a question to which the answer (which we do not
understand) is that all things are *created*, and created
out of nothing – all this is *also* one way of telling an
ancient and sophisticated story: a story which can only
be learned, and its truth and adequacy tested and
explored, by participation in cultural contexts which
entertain it and which, perhaps, endorse it, embodying
it in social practices.

We might put it this way: to learn that we are
creatures, and that all things are created, and created
out of nothing, *takes time*. It took the Jewish and then
the Christian tradition many centuries. The story of this
learning process is, of course, the history of Jewish and
Christian doctrines of God, and there is no general
agreement amongst scholars as to how this story is best
told. Nineteenth-century German scholars gave
astonishingly confident accounts of what they called
'the history of religions', according to some of which,
throughout the human race, monotheism evolved out
of polytheism and, according to others, 'one finds
everywhere a decline from monotheism to
polytheism'.[15] Today, this confidence has evaporated:
we now know enough about the sheer diversity of
human cultures to mistrust any such single, all-
embracing narrative description of the way that things
have been.

Where the history, specifically, of Judaism is
concerned, it was once assumed that the many names of
God in the Old Testament are traces of an earlier
polytheism. This may be so, but it is no less plausible to
suppose that the Lord of Israel 'has many names,
because he cannot be known in the fashion of a
nameable individual' (as Moses soon found out).[16]

Is the God of Israel first known as the one who 'brought you out of Egypt' and then, eventually, the liberator becomes identified with the maker of the world – or was it the other way round? Once again, the simpler versions of *both* these stories have been abandoned. According to some recent scholarship, the best that we can do, at present, is 'to suppose that the historical narratives of entering into, breaking and restoring of covenants with God are set within an assumed framework of cosmic order, rather than that the latter is an extrapolation from historical order'.[17] (There is, I understand, considerable support for the view that the 'non-name', if we may call it that, given to Moses on Mount Horeb designates the giver as creator.)

It is, however, a far cry from 'frameworks of cosmic order', in general, to the specific conviction that all things are created *ex nihilo*. Whatever the details of the history, it remains the case that learning that all things are created, and created out of nothing, takes time. Moreover, there is a sense in which each generation, and indeed each individual, has to take the time to learn this for themselves – has to grow (or fail to grow) into some understanding of what it *means* to be created out of nothing: to be, from birth to death, and in every fibre of one's being, absolutely dependent on the mystery that we call God.

Pascal's not unreasonable terror before the silence of the skies is an indication of how difficult it is to learn to accept, and find our freedom in, our creaturehood, our radical dependence. The acknowledgement of finitude is acknowledgement of vulnerability, and this is something we are loth to do. The contingency or dependence of the creature is refracted in the network of mutual dependence which constitutes the world. In spite of their free subjectivity, says Karl Rahner, human beings experience themselves as being at the disposal of others, a disposal over which they have no control.

They never realize completely their possibilities in the world and in history. In an ultimate and inescapable way, human beings as doers and makers are still receiving and being made.[18]

In the darkness of the world the way things actually are, the mutual dependence between creatures is all too often experienced as (to echo Hegel) 'lordship and bondage', slavery and domination. As a result, it is not surprising that many people, especially when it is insisted, quite correctly, that the Creator is all-powerful, 'almighty', suspect that the condition of the creature is that of *absolute* slavery. Against which, not unreasonably, they rebel.

The root of the problem here, however, is not the notion of absolute dependence, but the unstated image of God as tyrant, as a very large and very powerful creature. As Karl Rahner put it, in 1961: 'For a really Christian doctrine of the relationship of the world to God, the autonomy of the creature does not grow in inverse but in direct proportion to the degree of the creature's dependence on, and belonging to God.'[19] In other words, the closer the relationship of the creature to the Creator, the more the creature grows in reality, in self-possession, and in freedom. Here is Karl Rahner again: human beings 'come to the real truth about themselves precisely by the fact that they patiently endure and accept this knowledge that their own reality is not in their own hands'.[20] Archbishop Rowan Williams says something very similar. 'Being creatures', he says, 'is learning humility, not as submission to an alien will, but as the acceptance of limit and death; *for* that acceptance, with all that it means in terms of our moral imagination and action, we are equipped by learning, through the grace of Christ and the concrete fellowship of the Spirit, that God is', in a phrase of Sebastian Moore's, 'the desire by which all live'.[21]

Of course, such acknowledgement of finitude, such 'acceptance of limit', requires, amongst other things, a reconstruction of contemporary accounts of freedom as the *absence* of limits and constraints. To be truly free, on some of these accounts, is to *have* what you want, and to *do* what you want, and to *say* what you want, and, from moment to moment, to *be* whoever and whatever you decide, that day, to be.

There are, fortunately, more rational accounts to hand. 'What,' asks Robin Kirkpatrick, 'does Dante mean by freedom?' His answer is to the effect that, in the *Inferno*, Dante shows what he does *not* mean: shows that freedom is 'not the breaking of bounds, still less irresponsibility towards others'. Then, in the *Purgatorio*, he develops his positive account. In the course of the *Purgatorio*, Dante (by which I now mean the character in Dante's narrative)

> slowly ... recognizes that the disciplines of purgation are not restrictions but the means by which the individual places himself in relation to other beings – both divine and human. Law becomes Love; and freedom finally is seen to reside in that interdependence of all beings which is fully enjoyed in Paradise.[22]

To learn *that* lesson is, of course, to grow in holiness and wisdom.

Courtesy and Reverence

A few years ago, I was conducting a doctoral seminar in Duke University, in North Carolina. One day, I was waxing eloquent on what is, I think, the central theme of this final chapter: namely, the indispensability, for the human creature's appropriate relationship to the Creator, of resolute attentiveness, of wonder, of contemplativity, of silence. One of my students, a very gifted Brazilian Baptist, said that *silence* hardly seemed to be a feature of the worship, in black Baptist churches, with which she was most familiar!

Her intervention was very helpful, in directing the seminar towards a deeper exploration of the way the metaphor of silence works: both the silence of human beings, listening in the darkness of the world, and the silence of the One who makes and heals all things through utterance of His Word.

The heart of the matter, I suggest, is that the contrary to the kind of silence that I have in mind is not *sound*, but *noise*. If human beings are (to take the title of the young Karl Rahner's doctoral dissertation) 'hearers of the word', it is by utterance, and hence by sound, that we are *constituted* – and constituted to be, in every fibre of our being, turned towards, attentive to, the voice that makes us and that calls us home. The self-utterance that God is spills over, we might say, into the making of the world. Sound is outgoing: speech and song are for communication, for relationship, for building up communion in the Spirit.

Noise, on the other hand, is egotistical. We make a noise in order to keep other people quiet; we make a noise in order to frighten off our enemies; we make a noise in order to drown out, by the din we make, the darkness and the terror of our hearts.

There are, I am sure, far better ways of putting it, but I hope that I have at least given an indication of why I said that the contrary of the constituting silence appropriate to 'hearers of the word', the silence that is *attentiveness* – to God and to each other – is, not sound, but noise, cacophony (to echo the theme of the previous chapter).

It would follow, surely, that at the very heart and centre of any scheme of Christian education would be the task of teaching each other to be still, to be attentive, to learn to acquire the courage to be quiet. I must, however, emphasize that, in saying this, I am *not* speaking about 'spirituality' – as this is too often, these days, understood.

When people say (as they do, it seems, with increasing frequency) that they are more interested in 'spirituality' than in 'religion', they usually seem to mean that they prefer the balm of private fantasy, the aromatherapy of uplifting individual sentiment, to the hard work of thought and action, the common struggle to make sense of things, to redeem and heal the world. When church leaders are exhorted to concentrate on 'spiritual' affairs, the implication sometimes seems to be that these things are different from, and loftier than, such mundane matters as proclaiming good news to the poor and setting at liberty those who are oppressed.

On the contrary, in suggesting that Christianity should be a kind of school of silence, an academy of attentiveness, I am suggesting that our task, as Christians, is to help each other to acquire the courage to be still, to keep our eyes open in the dark. Gethsemane would be the paradigm of the attentiveness we need. In the garden, Christ remained attentive to the Father's silence – while the disciples, unfortunately, slept.

That is, perhaps, a good place to end. In an interview which he gave on German television in 1976, Karl Rahner was asked: 'Could you briefly formulate the purpose and theme of your book, *Foundations of Christian Faith*?' His reply may serve as my conclusion: 'I really only want to tell the reader something very simple. Human persons in every age, always and everywhere, whether they realize and reflect upon it or not, are in relationship with the unutterable mystery of human life that we call God. Looking at Jesus Christ the crucified and risen one, we can have the hope that now in our present lives, and finally after death, we will meet God as our own fulfilment.'[23]

Notes

1   Mark 14: 36.
2   Job 38: 1.

3   Christoph Theobald, '"God is Relationship": Some
    Recent Approaches to the Mystery of the Trinity',
    Concilium 2001/1, p. 55.

4   Cardinal Nicholas of Cusa's treatise *De Docta
    Ignorantia* may have been issued only in 1440, but the
    theological impulse behind the work is older than
    Christianity itself, lying deep in the history of Jewish
    thought.

5   Blaise Pascal, *Pensées*, edited by Francis Kaplan (Paris:
    Editions du Cerf, 1992), 3.206.

6   See Nicholas Lash, 'Attending in Wonder to the World',
    Science and Theology: Twin Sisters, edited by Niels
    Henrik Gregersen, Kees van Kooten Niekerk and Knud
    Ochsner (Aarhus: University of Aarhus Press, 2002),
    pp. 1–24.

7   Carl Sagan, 'Introduction' to Stephen Hawking, *A Brief
    History of Time*, p. x (my stress).

8   Genesis 1: 1–2 (New Revised Standard Version).

9   'Je n'avais pas besoin de cette hypothèse-là.' The famous
    remark is a simplification of Laplace's reply to
    Napoleon, who had been defending a Newtonian
    theology (the date is 8 August 1802). Laplace was not
    affirming an atheism: he was simply insisting, against
    Newton and Napoleon, 'that the principles of mechanics
    must be mechanical', not theological (see Michael
    Buckley, *At the Origins of Modern Atheism*, p. 325).

10 Hermann Brück, 'Astrophysical Cosmology', in
    Cosmology and Theology, edited by David Tracy and
    Nicholas Lash, *Concilium* 166 (1983), pp. 45, 47.

11 Williams, *On Christian Theology*, p. 68 (his stress).

12 See Aquinas, *Summa Theologiae*, Ia, 44.

13 G.W.F. Hegel, *Lectures on the Philosophy of Religion. I*,
    edited by Peter C. Hodgson (Berkeley: University of
    California Press, 1984), p. 258.

14 *Summa Theologiae*, Ia, 1. 1. ad 2.

15 John Milbank, 'History of the One God', *Heythrop
    Journal, XXXVIII* (1997), pp. 371–400; p. 372.

16 Art. cit., p. 378.

17 Art. cit., p. 383.

18 See Karl Rahner, *Foundations of Christian Faith. An
    Introduction to the Idea of Christianity*, translated by
    William V. Dych (London: Darton, Longman and Todd;
    and New York: Seabury Press, 1978), p. 42.

19 Rahner, 'Thoughts on the Possibility of Belief Today',
    Theological Investigations, V, translated by Karl-H.

Kruger (Baltimore: Helicon Press; and London: Darton, Longman and Todd, 1966), p. 12.

20 Rahner, *Foundations*, p. 43.

21 Williams, *On Christian Theology*, p. 78, citing Sebastian Moore, *The Inner Loneliness* (London: Darton, Longman and Todd; and New York: Crossroads, 1982), p. 117.

22 Robin Kirkpatrick, *The Divine Comedy* (Cambridge: Cambridge University Press, 1987), p. 77.

23 Karl Rahner, *Karl Rahner in Dialogue. Conversations and Interviews, 1965–1982*, ed. Paul Imhof and Hubert Biallowons; translation edited by Harvey D. Egan (New York: Crossroad, 1986), p. 147.

Index of Proper Names
and Biblical References